MW00435875

Diving in
Stilettos First

Printed and Distributed by BookBaby. Pennsauken, NJ

Printed in the United States of America 2017 – 1st Edition

Cover Art By: Ian Barry, IG: @agent_yin_draws

Cover Design By: Jackie Navarro

Edited by: Elizabeth A. Bell

Follow me on Instagram: @Diving_In_Stilettos_First

Follow me on Twitter: @DiveNStilettos1

www.divinginstilettosfirst.com

ISBN 978-1-54390-640-0 (pbk)

ISBN 978-1-54390-641-7 (ebook)

Diving in Stilettos First

MEMOIRS OF DATING MR. RIGHT NOW

SHAUNTAY L. DUNBAR

Diving in Stilettos

Acknowledgments

First and foremost I would like to thank God. It is through HIM all things are possible. Everything you go through in life is for a reason. It is to prepare you for your time. When God says it's your time there's no running from it, there's no more postponing, there's no saying no. HE wants wonderful things for you. You just have to believe you deserve those wonderful things and open your arms to receive them.

Thank you to all of my amazing friends. When you have goals in life, you have to surround yourself with like-minded people. I have certainly done that. I admire each and every one of you. Thank you all for your support and encouragement. Krystal Barbosa, Bobby & Chantel Butler, Todd Davis, Joe Dougé, Jonathan Elmore, Rachel Espersen, Tyla Fernandez, Elleser Galleta, Caroline Hedaya, Kodjo Hogan, Brian James, Sherice Lezama, Stedson McIntyre, Enersy Mendez, Jackie Navarro, Zuleika Pena, Natalie Sanchez, Audrey Sanders, and Niema Washington. I love you guys.

To my girls, my boy, my sisters, the people who have become family: my best friends Samantha Baxter, Stephanie Cole, Jamika Mack, Valarie Nicholas, Nichola Pointer, Rodney Skerrett, and Nicole Winkfield. You all have been in my life for a long time, some of you at least 30 years. I have learned so much from each of you and I am so grateful to have you in my life still. Thank you for listening to my crazy stories, thank you for sharing

5

the tears and the laughter. Thank you for never judging and always telling it like it is. You are remarkable people and I am blessed to call you my extended family.

I would like to give a special thank you to my newest friend Lakesha Baker. I feel really blessed to have met you. I admire your strength and beautiful spirit. Thank you for all of your advice, support, and encouraging words throughout this process. You are truly remarkable.

Thank you Kyle Flowers for being patient with me, cheering for me, being supportive of me, believing in me, hugging me and never letting me forget my goals. Your persistence and ambition is admirable. I appreciate you more than you'll ever know. Thank you for being you. Love you. #supercornydope

Thank you to all of my supportive co-workers. You all know exactly who you are! Xoxo

Thank you to my family for their continuous love and support. I am blessed to have grown up in such an affectionate home with such loving people. Thank you for always being there for me. Thank you for loving me unconditionally and believing in me. Lucinda Dunbar, Joseph Dunbar, Tyrone Hodge, Joseph White, Tyrone Hodge Jr., Baby Liam, Celeste Forde, Valerie White, Anita Pinto, Jacqueline Simpson, Corissa Harris, and Adrienne Hayes. I couldn't mention everyone, but I love all of you.

Last but certainly not least, I have to thank the woman who has always been my #1 fan, who raised me to be the woman I am today: My Mother Rhonda White. You have taught me to never compromise my dignity, to always walk with my head held high no matter what, and to celebrate the fact that I am one of a kind. You've always seen the greatness in your children and you never let us forget that. I admire your strength, your sense of self, your independence, and your ability to put your family first. You were my first role model, and let me tell you, I am honored to be your daughter. I will always strive for excellence because you worked too hard for me not to. I hope I've made you proud. I love you mommy.

Diving in Stilettos

Table of Contents

Introduction…

Chapter 1: Vegas…The trouble with Sin City

Chapter 2: Can't Get Right

Chapter 3: BagelBoy Break

Chapter 4: Superman…The History of my Cuddy Buddy

Chapter 5: Adventures with StickyFingers

Chapter 6: Online Dating Round 1 - Applebee'sKing

Chapter 7: Blocking the DramaKing

Chapter 8: The Hook-Up…Introduction to StrawSipper

Chapter 9: The Hook Up…My date with StrawSipper

Chapter 10: A New Year & Online Dating Again: Chef OnALedge & Dr.NoNotReally

Chapter 11: Framed aka Mr. Modest

Chapter 12: Happy Birthday Framed

Chapter 13: Deal or No Deal

Diving in Stilettos

Introduction

My name is Shauntay Lucinda Dunbar and I am a writer. That was literally the first time I've ever typed that sentence and let me tell you, it feels amazing. I am 35 years old and was born and raised in Bronx, New York. I went to Morgan State University in Baltimore, Maryland and graduated in 2003 with my Bachelors in Marketing. Currently I am an event planner for a luxury publisher and I absolutely love what I do. I've been planning events since college; I enjoy the preparation behind the scenes and watching it all come together. Makes sense that I would enjoy the process of self-publishing my first book.

Diving in Stilettos First is a true story about my actual dating life over the past 5 years. Shaunie is my nickname used by family and close friends. It provides a level of comfort for me so I call myself Shaunie throughout the book. Every scenario in this book actually happened. Every character is a real human with real feelings, so I have opted to change the names to protect the innocent.

Being a single woman in New York City has taught me a lot about myself. I finally understand that nothing worth having comes easy. I've learned to embrace all of my struggles and laugh at myself quite often. Each experience has made me stronger and certainly made me appreciate my wins so much more. When you earn the things you receive, no one can take it away from you.

Trust me when I say there is an ultimate comfort in knowing that.

I have plenty of goals for the future and plan to achieve every one. I'm no stranger to the grind. I work on being the best possible me every day and I hope I inspire others to do the same. When you are secure with who you are as a person, your opportunities are limitless. I'm ready to step into my purpose and pay it forward. You can't grow as a person and not share what you've learned. God didn't give you your gift so you could keep it to yourself.

Chapter 1: Vegas...The Trouble with Sin City

It is 2015 and summertime in New York. As I sit at my desk at work I think to myself, "Self, what are you doing with your life?" I'm a single 34-year-old woman living alone in the greatest city on earth, NYC. I wish I can say my life was all champagne toasts and trips to the Hamptons, but alas it is not. (Not yet anyway.) Currently I am working 2 jobs to make ends meet. The original goal was to pay off debt, get back to working one job, marry an amazing man, have two children, no pets (I don't care for the cleanup), live in my beautiful condo in Westchester County and be happy. Well the only part of that sentence that has happened so far is that I'm happy...for the most part.

Let's rewind and start right around the time in my life where my world was flipped upside down. Autumn 2011: my annulment was finalized. Why an annulment you wonder? I'm technically Catholic, but that's another story for another time. Anyway, I was married for almost 3 years to someone who was clearly not my soul mate. He tells me on my 30th birthday he doesn't want to have any more children. He had one child from a previous relationship, I had none. He knew that would be a deal breaker for me and I would not be able to compromise on that.

Even though I was not 100% happy in my marriage, I always thought, "Hey you make your bed you lie in it." I spent 7 years of my life with Diablo. I want to say I regret every single minute I spent with that man, but I don't. Experience is the best teacher. He was not the best husband. To be real, I was not the best wife because I was not the best me. I can say that now that I've grown. You can't stay married to someone who never truly felt the same about you as you did about them. I believe he proposed because he thought he was at the age where he "should" be married. He "should" have a wife and take on that responsibility. He proposed, not because that was what he'd always wanted for himself, but because he "should" want those things for himself. Who wants to be the old guy hitting on girls at the club right? My logic prevents me from hating his guts.

We were a couple for 3 years and living together before the proposal. We had broken up once briefly, because he told me he never saw himself getting married. That was my cue to pack my shit and get out of dodge. I loved him dearly, but I was not about to continue to play house forever. I never realized how many lies he told me just to keep me around, until it was over. There was love there, but I can't tell you what kind. He courted me all over again and won me back. He proposed in Bryant Park. Tears of joy streamed down my face. He finally realized I was the one (or so I thought).

After you spread the news that you're engaged, you should certainly pay attention to people's reactions. My mother was definitely not overjoyed about the news, but she saw how happy I was and got on board. My Granny was undeniably elated. My friends were shocked, but happy that I was happy. It wasn't until I announced my marriage was over that all the real feelings about it came out. My mom never liked him. She thought he was sneaky. My friends were surprised I liked him from the beginning. We didn't match as a couple and he dimmed my shine. I didn't have my normal pep or my get up and go attitude. I had turned into a homebody. I loved to travel and he was afraid of airplanes. I loved to eat out (but anything outside of Spanish food and kid cuisine made his stomach hurt) and he didn't like to use public restrooms. We went to the movies a lot, but that died down when he came to the conclusion that just waiting for the film to come out on Blu-Ray would be more cost effective. "We're going to own the movie anyway," he would say.

I'll never forget the day I realized I was married to the wrong man. It was about 1 year into the marriage and we were headed to the movies as usual. We saw this old couple coming down the block. The husband was proudly pushing his wife in her wheelchair. It brought me back to the night before my wedding. I was at my mother's house and we were having a little mother - daughter chat. She asked, "God forbid if something ever happened to Diablo and he was bound to a wheelchair for the rest of his life, do you know what you would do?" I replied, "I would be sad, but I'd help him with his physical therapy and I would be pushing his ass all over New York City." Me and my mom hugged and laughed hysterically. I think that was the longest hug my mother had ever given me. Naturally, seeing this couple reminded me of that moment with my mom. So I posed the question. "Babe if God forbid I was bound to a wheelchair what would you do?" Diablo said, "Ugh, I don't know. Nobody has time to deal with that shit. I'd hire somebody to watch you I guess. I'd have to go to work. Those bills would be expensive as shit." Needless to say all I could think was: What the hell have I done?

Well, time has taught me that you will never find true happiness just lying around dwelling in the past. It was a tough decision to end my union, but I don't regret it. I've learned so much about me these past 4 years that my comfort level of knowing myself is at an all-time high. I can't look back because I'm so curious to see what the future has in store for me.

So let's back track to me getting my groove back. I am in the summer of 2011 and newly single. This was the first time I've been single in 16 years. I didn't know what to do with myself. I had moved back in with my Granny, sleeping on an airbed, and still going to work every day like life was peachy keen. It's so funny how when one part of your life is a complete mess, you become a superstar in the part of your life that is still running fairly smooth. I got to work early, sharing ideas to improve business, and volunteering to help lighten the boss's load. In my professional life, I was a stellar performer. In my personal life, I was a confused mess.

While on a business trip in Las Vegas I shared my failed marriage story with my closest co-worker. Needless to say her jaw dropped. She was amazed at how poised I remained the entire time and expressed how much she admired my strength.

Kelly Cutrone said it best: "Sometimes, if not most of the time, you find out who you are by figuring out who and what you're not."[1] I know I am not a settler. I know I'm not a loser. I know I am not passive. I didn't know what God had in store for me and well, I still don't know, but it is certainly something great. Everything that I have been through has led me to this moment and I have to keep pushing because HE's not done with me yet.

So I'm giving my all at work and everyone knows about "the death" of my marriage. I've repeated the story at least 100 times. I became so good at telling the story it became stand-up comedy to me. I got my happy back and that dark moment in time no longer dimmed my shine. I voluntarily bring it up if I feel it will help someone. Other than that, it's forward movement to infinity and beyond.

Can someone tell me how your exes tend to know when you are back on the market? I was never big on sharing my life with social media, especially my relationship status. So when these guys started randomly sending emails and making calls, it could only mean one thing. The wolves picked up my new freedom scent.

Single life was short lived. My ex from grade school reached out and low and behold I was willing and curious to know what his life was about these days. Vegas and I always had an intense connection. When we weren't arguing over something ridiculous, we were laughing, joking, and tearing each other's clothes off. Angry or not, sex is where we found our common ground. We were like frenemies in a sense. When it was good it was great, but when it was bad it was terrible.

After long chats with Vegas, it turned out that in a few weeks I would be in his neck of the woods for work. We would see each other for the first time in maybe 2-3 years. Vegas offered to take me out and show me the town since I had a free evening. He showed up to my hotel room and when I opened the door I was slightly shocked. His eyebrows were arched almost better than mine, he had this "mohawkish" style haircut, his clothes were fitted, and he wore TOMS. Clearly living in Sin City made him lose his NYC flare. He was very metrosexual. He looked extremely nervous or it could have just been the Jersey Shore eyebrows. He had always been a little guy, but always had an athletic build. It was great to see he had kept himself up even though he was a little too pretty for me.

We went out and had a drink. He told me how he ended up in Sin City and what his goals were in life. I have to say the man was in the right business: sales! He was selling me on his dream and had me hanging on his every word. I started thinking about what life would be like living in this city. Perhaps I could go to culinary school and open my bakery or work in a hotel selling event space. The options for this city were limited in my eyes, but he made me believe there were endless possibilities. After a few more drinks and eating some appetizers we headed back to my hotel room and certainly relived our younger days.

I felt like such a "bad girl." Although broken-up and moved on, legally I was still married. How could I have possibly slept with another man? One thing I knew for sure, I had a great business trip and that metrosexual still had it. We continued speaking and I made another trip out there. This time he put me in a hotel and I was spoiled with gifts and dinners. It was great. I wanted to go out and see another part of Sin City. There were casinos and strip clubs everywhere, but I wanted to see the livable side.

He took me to this outdoor mall. There were lots of stores that I drooled over like Chanel and Louis Vuitton. It was late in the evening and the stores were closing so I couldn't go inside. We went into this restaurant lounge where he insisted I have their signature blue drink. I thought it was gross. Vegas thought it was amazing. That college frat boy life would never leave him. He still drank like a fish.

We ended up sitting in a booth, and with piercingly loud music playing in the background he professed his love. At this point we were dating for about 2 months and he was ready to date exclusively. I just got this new found freedom and he wanted to take it away already...so annoying! He had asked before, but this was, I guess, his "gentleman way" of making me his woman. I wasn't ready for this, but he told me, "Shaunie, I want to give you the world. Make all your dreams come true. We work together as a team. You help me now and I will help you later. You move out here and we will build a life. I'm not going to ask you again!" I said, "Okay." "Okay what?" he asks. I said, "You said you weren't going to ask me again and I'm okay with that." Surprisingly, he called me a dick. I never laughed so hard in my

19

life. In my 30 years of living I had never been called a dick, well not to my face anyway. I said, "Look, this is my first time being single as an adult. I'm staying with my Granny. I really feel like I need to live on my own for a little while before I can commit to anyone. Besides, I'm still legally married and it would be weird having an estranged husband and a pretty boyfriend... just saying. When my annulment goes through and if you still like me, we will make something work." To my surprise, my tap dancing was well-received and it bought me some time to think about where I wanted this relationship to go.

Back at home I needed to make more money so I could move. I honestly feel I have the best grandma in the world. She means well and once her baby, always her baby. I could talk to her about anything and she never judges. Granny always gives sound advice... on most topics, and she's super cool, but I find that we get along so much better when I live somewhere else. After the 3rd argument about me not eating the food she made for dinner, I decided I needed a second job and fast. I already pawned my wedding ring and other relationship jewelry. That covered the 2 months' rent and 1 month security, but I would need to save more in order to have a cushion, not just enough to survive. This girl wanted to live. So I applied to work part-time at a gym to get a little extra money.

Working at the gym was great. I had a cool young manager. The sales guys were nice, but extremely full of themselves. My supervisor was a young Brooklyn girl with a good heart, but that brain of hers made a lot of crazy decisions. I think I may have become her therapist at some point with all the positive advice I gave out 4 times a week. I have to say, God will put people in your life as a lesson or a blessing. I learned a lot about myself being a mentor to this young lady. I hope she learned something as well. After a few months of working at the gym, it really took a toll on me. It ate up all my weekends and the money did not balance out the time and effort I was putting in to be there.

I was in a long distance relationship with Vegas and he called me at all times of night, not caring about the east coast / west coast time difference. My Granny was fearful of me traveling so late at night from working all these late hours. Her nagging about staying up past her bedtime because she was worried really irked my last nerve. I was paying for my car to stay in a garage because there is NO parking where my grandma lives, and on top of all of that I had to hear about my unofficial therapy patient's shenanigans. I needed a break. I needed to make this period in my life a little easier. Being the impatient Aries I am, I decided to find out if I could transfer to the gym located closer to my first job. This would be a quick fix, but unbeknownst to me not a solution for the bigger problem.

The new gym was lovely, sales people were friendly, trainers were really nice and funny, and the best part, it was only 3 blocks from my first job. This would be a lot easier for me. Well, when you are not supposed to be somewhere for too long, God will stir the pot. I got a tip from a former gym colleague that my young supervisor, aka therapy patient, would be transferring

to my new location. Why my new place of tranquility? I called the
front desk because I couldn't believe it and surprise, surprise it
was her on the other end. I went online and applied for
a seasonal position at Bloomingdales. It was time to move on.
Now don't get me wrong, my young supervisor was very sweet,
but self-esteem is something that cannot be taught. I tried many
times to convince her that her brain was the sexy body part that
would get her places. She needed to use it so she could make
better choices. I felt like a broken record; she would just have to
learn on her own.

Now at this point I have a long-distance boyfriend,
Vegas, who wants to know my every move. Trust issues are never
good for any relationship let alone a long-distance one. He
decided to be a good boyfriend and treated me to a trip to
Jamaica. What a beautiful island. I thought this was a way for us
to get back to our happy place and stop all the bickering. Well
that was short-lived. Day 2 of the trip we had a falling out. I
understand that when you are on vacation you act out. No one
knows you in this foreign land so you're free to act a fool. His
drinking was out-of-control. He was rude and embarrassing.
After a nap it was like he regrouped and we were back to having
a good time. In public we were an ideal couple. The island staff
loved us. Behind closed doors we were *War of the Roses.*

I went on the balcony because we just argued and this
jerk closes the balcony door and locks it. I was so mad, but my
pride would not let me stoop to his level of pettiness. After about
10 minutes he came out and apologized. I have to say the
remainder of the trip was really fun. Of course as payback for my

embarrassment, I made him buy all those expensive pictures they take of you during your resort stay and I kept them all. I know he was happy to send me back home.

Back to the grind, I was working 3 jobs briefly and Granny's gracious hospitality was wearing thin. Vegas and I were constantly arguing because I wasn't so gung ho about moving to his city. All I wanted was my own place and peace of mind. I convinced him that moving on my own would be the best thing for our future. I had to experience that at least once in my life. I honestly recommend that for all young women. It's the best way to learn about yourself and what you are capable of. He accepted my decision of living alone because, well, he was tired of arguing and he knows how stubborn I am.

I stalked Craigslist and came across this lovely apartment described so beautifully. It was a first floor corner apartment with exposures facing the front of the building. Already I was excited. During my marriage we lived in a ground floor apartment. We had to keep the shades down so people walking by on the street couldn't look inside our home. Usually I didn't look at listings without a picture, but it was something about the description. I did a quick Google search of the location and expressed my interest in the apartment. My mom came with me to check it out just in case it was a scam and she had to use her Louisville Slugger. The landlord was very sweet and we hit it off immediately.

On January 30, 2012 I got the keys and on January 31,

2012 I moved into my new apartment. It was mine all mine and I did it all on my own. It was a proud moment for me. I was back to having one job and I have to say I was pretty bored. I barely slept since I had to adhere to Vegas's time schedule. He worked 2 jobs so his free time was limited. I figured since I wasn't sleeping anyway, I should probably make some money. So I applied to an organizational store and started my part-time career as an overnight stock person.

The people I worked with were so fun and had all kinds of backgrounds. It was great. Little did I know that sharing fun stories about this new job would annoy the hell out of Vegas. He accused me of cheating on him with a co-worker. He told me he had people out in NYC watching me and I needed to stop lying to him. He was losing it. There was a co-worker I found extremely attractive, but it wasn't a big deal because all the ladies there thought he was hot. I have to be honest and say Vegas was getting on my nerves. He was always complaining. In fact he nagged so much I diagnosed myself with ADHD. I struggled trying to pay attention to his crap. He was out-of-sight and out-of-mind. All I wanted was peace. I had no choice but to set up boundaries.

I told him since he didn't respect my time, he could only call me before midnight east coast time. I was done with doing all the compromising. In my last relationship I was constantly bending over backwards trying to make someone else happy and, well, you see how that ended. I was in "selfish mode" and had to do what was best for me. He wasn't happy about my demands, but he met them as best he could. Unfortunately, it didn't put us in a good place. I was becoming this independent tyrant that couldn't be stopped.

I was taking care of my finances all by myself. I was even able to get discounts when getting my car serviced with my winning smile and charm (ha). I told Vegas about my special rates and he was not happy about that. Then I told him the car guy invited me to a block party in his old neighborhood. I asked if he knew about it and wanted to go. Vegas was pissed. Listen I was being nice. The guy was cool. I wasn't interested in him at all. What was the big deal anyway? I had nothing to hide. Not to mention Vegas wasn't paying for my car's upkeep. Hello! When we were in Jamaica he charmed his way into getting us a room upgrade, without one complaint from me. Maybe my eyes rolled, but nothing major. Discount charming was completely innocent.

Vegas decided it was time for him to see how I was living back in New York. It also gave him a chance to visit his old stomping grounds. I picked him up from the airport and he gave my car the side eye. I was driving a 2010 sedan and although he bragged of having a BMW, I remember remaining composed when we were waiting for his car in Sin City. The valet pulled up in a 1999 (I think) box BMW whose passenger door could only be opened from the inside. No judgment from me though. Vegas was my man and I was proud of him for having his own. Anyway, we arrived at my apartment and he dropped his stuff in the corner, while stating, "I'll be neat. I know how you get." I don't have OCD, but I do believe everything has a place.

I needed to go to Walmart to pick up a few things for the house and Vegas came with. While in the car he reclines his seat all the way back and takes a nap. We are literally 10 minutes away when he gets a call. I'm singing along to my music and I keep hearing him say, "Oh okay, mmm hmmm, word, interesting, mmm hmmm, okay good looking, thanks." He hangs up the phone, pops up into the upright position and goes off. "I fucking knew it. You think you slick. The oil change guy said he had you in the bag." I'm like wait a minute, WHAT? I had to calm my nerves from the surprise pop up that scared the hell out of me. I immediately put my hands at 10 and 2 on the steering wheel. I'm trying to figure out what the hell he's yelling about. I am so puzzled and he clearly doesn't care about his life, hitting the driver of a moving vehicle with such an element of surprise. "CT! Fucking CT is my brother's best friend!" he yells. "I'm sorry who is CT?" I ask calmly. "Calvin is the fucking oil change guy. Mr. Block Party said he's been buttering you up and it's only a matter of time before he takes you down." "WHAT? Okay first of all he's lying. Second, he has my number because it's in the computer system. He asked to take me to a steak place in Brooklyn and I said no I have a boyfriend," I say defending myself. "Did you tell him who your boyfriend was?" Vegas asked. "No, why would I say I have a boyfriend named Vegas? I declined the offer. You can't be serious right now." I was beginning to get pissed. "Take me home Shaunie. Take me to my mother's house right now," he yelled. "Okay can we at least go to Walmart first? We drove all this way. It's right here," I say, determined to get my Swiffer wipes. "I don't give a fuck where it is. Take me to my mother's house now. I'm not playing." "Okay FINE (still pulling into the Walmart parking lot) I just need to grab a couple of things and we can go. You can even stay in the car. Don't you want Doritos? You love Doritos. I'll get you some and you can take them to your mother's house," I say sweetly. "You make me sick (he grabs a cart). Hurry up," After about an hour in Walmart, with me being my bubbly self, I get everything I need including his Doritos and he's my friend again.

Turned out Vegas's family was throwing the block party and Mr. Oil Change guy was the DJ. Vegas was so out of touch with his family he had no idea they planned this neighborhood extravaganza. Well guess who wanted to go to the block party now. I don't know if he had something to prove or if he wanted to see how I would act around this lame oil changer. All I knew was it was his last day in NYC, so I was going to make the best of it. I couldn't wait to go home and get back to my peaceful life.

When we walked in, it was like he was a celebrity. It had been years since he was home and so everyone was so happy to see him. He was happy to know he was so loved and missed. He introduced me to everyone but the DJ (oh gee I wonder why). I wanted to knock all his records on the ground for lying; even better, I wanted to do one of those really dramatic scenes and bump the DJ table, breaking a record in half over my knee. Luckily for him I'm not that dramatic. When I have an audience I like to use the attention for good, not evil. The more social Vegas became, the more I faded into the background. I ended up

27

chatting with his mom and watching his little nieces and nephews play. The neglect didn't bother me. I'm a social butterfly. It was when I told him I was leaving and he said "okay bye" that I snapped back into reality. "Okay I'll just take the rest of your stuff out of my car and leave it on the curb. Have a safe flight." He follows me and says, "I was coming to walk you, but you're so fast. Lighten up."

He was so aggravating! How could I possibly date someone that gets under my skin so bad? It amazes my friends how I am able to find that little bit of good in someone and just hold on to it. I guess I just accepted that Vegas was not perfect, and it was either that I find beauty in his imperfections or I move out the way and let someone else find the beauty in his world of mess.

But this was the straw that broke the camel's back. Vegas and I were hardly communicating any more. When I called him he didn't answer and pretty much vice versa. The texts became very dry and I was losing interest. He went from working 2 jobs to 3 jobs. I've always admired his ambition and hustle, but he had a hard time admitting when he was in trouble or needed a little help. I feel like when you're in a relationship, your problems are mine just as your successes are mine and vice versa. If you are a secret squirrel and not sharing, I can't help you. Being mean and not explaining yourself just makes me think you're an asshole and I'm wasting my time.

At this point, it is a year into my first long-distance relationship and I was not happy. We had a huge argument about me not moving west again. I had no desire to anymore, and if he was going to be the only person I knew out there, it was not going to be a good move. I loved him very much, but I didn't like him at all. I didn't like who I was with him. I was always yelling, arguing, and just irritated. So after the last argument about the DJ, aka oil change guy, he decides he's not going to contact me. He wasn't returning my calls, text messages, nothing. Six whole days went by and this man didn't know if I was alive or dead. On Day 7 I get a text from him.

Vegas: *Hey.*

Now some of you may think this is petty of me, but I didn't reply. I was hurt and angry. On Day 8, I get a text from him again.

Vegas: *Hey babe! Just reply and let me know you're okay. If I don't hear from you I'm contacting your mother.*

I sent out a PSA to my mom, aunt, and anyone else whose number he may have had. Do not communicate with Vegas. Ignore and delete. My mom felt bad, but she knew whose team she was on. I let the weekend go by. I was working both jobs and didn't have the energy to break up with him. I told myself that Monday I would make the call and say goodbye. He called my job on Monday from a blocked number and I accidentally answered the phone. I was silent as he hit me with the sarcasm like it was my fault he ignored me for an entire week. He told me that I needed to learn a lesson. I said fine and we would discuss it further when I got home.

The running joke between us has been that he was always

the one to dump me. In grade school and after college he was the one that was the dumper. He thought it was hilarious how he could "dump me" and still get me back. Even after dating doctors and lawyers that were so "great," he still chose to date me. As if I should be honored. My, my, my how the tables were about to turn.

I called and he picked up right away. Needless to say he had an attitude and was being very short with me. So I began. "I just wanted to tell you how hurt I am to know that you could allow so much time to pass and not pick up the phone once. What if something happened to me while you were dishing out your 'lesson?' The fact that you were able to go that long and purposely not return my calls, shows me that you don't really care about me. Your pride and ego are way more important than I am and that's fine. I'm glad I know. We are over. I don't want to be in a relationship with someone who thinks of me as a child that needs to be 'taught a lesson.' I wish you the best of luck in all your endeavors, but don't you ever in this life time contact me again. I hope you learned from your own lesson." Then I held for the dramatic pause, heard nothing, and ended the call. I guess he was in shock. I felt free again, liberated. I stood up for myself and it felt great!

Steve Harvey says, "You don't lose a good man, you lose a man who's not good for you."2 Vegas and I were toxic together and I had to let go. Five minutes later my phone rang and it was him. I had to hit pause on my victory dance and put the serious face on. I decided to ignore the call and my victory dance resumed. Then the text messages came.

Vegas: *You don't understand. I was sick I had to get my finger nail removed it was infected.*

Vegas: *I was going deaf in one ear and had to stay in the hospital for them to run test. Thank God I'm okay.*

Vegas: *You're not being fair. You have to give us another chance.*

I'm not going to lie, I thought about it for 2 seconds then I blocked him and I continued my happy dance. About a week later I got a letter in the mail. It was from Vegas. He apologized for his behavior and really wanted us to try again. I cannot lie. I was touched by the gesture. No one writes letters anymore. I want to say I burned it or ripped it up and threw it in the air like confetti, but I didn't. I simply put it back in its envelope and left it on the table for weeks until it got lost in the shuffle of all the junk mail and disappeared. The letter made me not hate him or regret him. I learned a few things dating Vegas. I am not good with long distance relationships. You should never date someone who competes with you. More importantly, never let someone try to make you believe that they are the only person in the world that knows how great you are. When you believe in your greatness, others can't help but to believe in it too.

#

Chapter 2: Can't Get Right

It was the end of summer 2012 and it appeared that all I was doing was working. My event season for my 9 to 5 was kicking into high gear: I had 2 awards banquets, 4 trade shows and a seminar I needed to execute all the while working 3 nights a week at my overnight job. Talk about exhausted. I took a little break from the dating world. Vegas really drained me and I wasn't sure how ready I would be to meet a brand new person. Last time I met someone new, I ended up marrying Diablo, a mama's boy with no ambition and no driver's license.

I started thinking about high school and how everything was so simple then. Oh how I missed the days when my bills consisted of nails, hair, cell phone, and shoes. In high school, my boyfriend was a star athlete: 6'3", playing varsity basketball, and FINE. He was in a grade higher than mine, went to a different school, and I talked about how great he was all the time. We met on a youth retreat to Washington DC. I was 1 of 12 students chosen to experience life abroad and got a chance to live in Mexico for 3 weeks. He was supposed to go to Mexico as well, but my bad boy got in trouble and was only allowed to attend the DC weekend retreat. We were both shy and flirted the entire weekend. I watched him play basketball, he sat next to me during group discussions, and we took a ton of pictures. I was so in love when I came back from that trip. I told my mother all about him immediately. The look of nervousness on her face as she smiled and listened to my every word was priceless. I think that was the longest cab ride for her. He and I dated on and off throughout high school but when he went away to college, he lost his mind. Some people can't handle that kind of freedom. I can't even begin to count how many universities he attended. One thing's for sure, despite all the trouble he got into, he kept going to school somehow some way, but just couldn't get himself all the way together.

On my lunch break I called my bestie. "Sistaaaaaa," Robyn sings. "Hey sunshine," I reply. Since high school and even now, we never know how to simply say "hello how are you?" to one another like civilized young ladies. "Sooo I have a mission. I need to find Can't Get Right." "What? Why?" Robyn responds with a big sigh and I'm pretty sure she rolled her eyes. It didn't faze me one bit. Robyn was always down for my shenanigans. I told her I needed to know what he was up to. I wanted to know if he was married with kids, rich living the glamorous life, and more importantly, had he forgot all about me. So being the genius she is she says, "Did you try Google?" "Duh, this is why I talk to you; let me do it right now. It appears he works as a basketball coach for a girls' team in Harlem. I'm going!" I say without hesitation. "Um, maybe you should call first and confirm he actually works there before you go popping up like a crazy person," Robyn suggests. My best friend was one smart cookie. "Okay I'll call you back," I say as I continue my Google detective work. I wanted to see if I could find a recent picture. After dealing with metrosexual eyebrows I was done with the element of a surprise face to face. I had no luck finding a picture so I called the rec center where he was coaching. "Hi I'm looking to place my daughter in your basketball program. Can you tell me the name of the coach? You can never be too careful these days you know what I'm saying." "Can't Get Right is our head coach. He's great with the girls and the parents love him. Everyone does really. He's here every Tuesday and Thursday." "Thank you so much." I squealed and did a little victory twirl in my chair. I called Robyn and told her Operation: Can't Get Right was under way and I needed something to wear and a kid.

The plan was to arrive unsuspected. My friend Victoria volunteered her daughter Brittany as the basketball camp prospect. Brittany is such a girly-girl, so I wasn't too sure she would be believable, but she was adorable and available. We were going to take a tour around the gym and casually bump into him like a "oh my, what are you doing here?" kind of thing. He would look amazing, smell like a fresh dose of yes, take me out to dinner, and we would live happily ever after. Sounded like a good plan to me. The director of the gym told me to come around 6pm so that's exactly what I did. I showed up on Tuesday dressed adorably in a flared skirt and tight v neck tee shirt. The girls were very up and perky in the shirt so I had to do a quick shimmy to make sure they wouldn't accidentally pop out if I needed to bend over. No worries I was still very classy.

I walked in looking around and slowly turned my head to lock eyes with the front desk person. Dramatic entrance, but nope it wasn't him. It was this little girl learning reception. She asked if I needed help and I told her I wanted to take a tour before I signed my niece up for basketball. She said, "Oh okay you can go ahead." Just like that? You just let strangers come in and walk around? Note to self: My future child is never coming here. Victoria and I gave each other the "what the hell" eye stare and proceeded up the steps. No Can't Get Right. We go to the weight room, the pool area, the yoga room, and finally we find the basketball gym. Little girls were doing drills and there were a few really tall guys in there, but none were Can't Get Right. I saw this little girl resting on the wall near the door so I said, "Hey sunshine, is Coach Can't Get Right here today?" She looked me up and down and said, "No he'll be back next Tuesday. You looking to sign up?" I sensed a hint of sarcasm, but I didn't engage. I don't like rude children. I simply gave a quick smile and said, "No, but Thank you." Listen: I'm not afraid to fight a kid. She was tall, but I could have taken her. As I left I thought to myself, damn I have to do this all over again. Brittany was booked next week (she had a piano lesson). I couldn't show up alone, I would look like a creep. So I called my girl Nadia. "Hey girl I need to borrow Isabell."

The following Tuesday, Nadia and Isabell met me at the recreation center. Isabell looked adorable (I had another girly-girl on my hands). "Isabell, let's practice. 'So little girl, do you like basketball?'" Isabell answered, "Not really, my mom made me come." "Cut, cut, cut! That was not a part of the script. You love basketball so much, you can't wait to join the team and get some ice cream afterward," I say enthusiastically. Isabell says, "Make it P.F. Chang's and we got a deal." This kid was good; really good.

We start walking across the street and there he is. He walked out with 2 trash bags and kids jumping all over him asking if they could sign out equipment. I'm standing there in my orange dress as the sunlight is hitting every angle on me perfectly and I say, "Hello Can't Get Right." It was simple and powerful. I gave myself a high five in my head. He stared at me as if he had seen a ghost and says, "Is it really you? Are you real?" I giggled thinking he was joking, but he was so serious. I said, "You work here, that's so crazy!" He smiled and said, "Yes I get off at 9. I want to hug you so bad, but I'm dirty and you look so beautiful and clean." I told him we could hug later when he gets off from work and we could catch up. He looked the same, well minus the dusty rec center uniform. I told him Isabell wanted to play basketball. He turns to her and says, "Hello pretty lady. You like basketball?" Isabell says, "Yes a little, but I love P.F. Chang's." Nadia and I were laughing hysterically.

My friend Jada lived in the area so we decided to go kill time at her apartment until Can't Get Right got off from work. Jada decided we should look at his Facebook while we waited. "Ladies, man your stations we have a recent post stand by for upload," Jada yells. Can't Get Right put up a picture of us from when we were 16 years old and the caption read: "She's back I can't believe she's back." All three of us looked at each other and said, "How'd he find that old picture that fast?" The jokes flew all over the room. Does he keep it in his wallet? Is it a screen saver? Does it hang in his work locker? My friends are hilariously brutal. Shortly thereafter I shush the room. Can't Get Right was calling my phone. He told me he got off in 10 minutes and wanted to know where I would like to meet. Nadia and I left our cars parked in front of the rec center, so we had to walk back that way anyway. I told him we would meet him there.

We start walking over and Isabell is holding my hand telling me about school, her plans for the rest of the summer and what she usually orders from P.F. Chang's when he walked up. Isabell says, "Hello Coach." I just have to say this little girl is going places in life. She is awesome. Nadia and Isabell get in their car, while Can't Get Right and I stand in front of my car and continue talking.

He tells me he has a daughter and I felt a sharp pain in my chest as I smiled and said, "A daughter? Wow that's…wow! How old? She's 5? What? Wow good for you huh, look at you somebody's Father." As he told me how smart and beautiful she was I couldn't help but be pissed off. How dare he breed with another woman? That should have been our daughter. He's totally screwing up the perfect fantasy I created in my head. Diablo had a kid and his child's mother was a nightmare. I was not, absolutely not dealing with that again. No way was I dealing with some crazy woman that wants to make his life hell because he doesn't want to be with her. First red flag shot up. "Damn it man!" I say out loud. "What happened, are you okay?" he asked. "Yeah, I'm fine. I had some spicy food earlier. It must be heart burn." I was surprised I was able to say a made up excuse considering the size of the lump in my throat. He told me that his mother just got back from Chicago and would love to see me. He

37

asked if I would like to go see her. I thought it was late in the night, but he swore it would be fine so I went with it.

We get to the apartment building and boy does it bring back old memories. Me arriving in the cab and him coming downstairs to pay for it, he and I cuddling in the court yard talking about any and everything. Everything looked the same; even the doorman Mr. Stevens was still there. We go upstairs and Can't Get Right uses his key to open the door. I think to myself that's not strange right? Lots of adults still have keys to their parent's home...right? We walk in and there's his mom ready to greet me with a big smile and open arms. Ms. Lana was my favorite. Even after Can't Get Right and I broke up, Ms. Lana and I kept in touch. I would go visit her and his grandmother. We would be sitting in the living room, eating Entenmann's cake, watching *Oprah*, and Can't Get Right would come in shocked to see me.

After college I had to break up with Ms. Lana. I told her it would be weird when her son finally got a serious girlfriend. There's no way he would be happy seeing me with her on the couch slicing another piece of Louisiana Crunch cake. It was sad, but she understood. "Where have you been young lady? I missed you so much, still gorgeous. I bet you have a fancy job don't you? Tell me everything," Ms. Lana says smiling. I told Ms. Lana about me being an event planner for 7 years with a luxury publisher and how I travel often for work, no kids, had my own apartment, and how Mr. Stevens let me park my car right in the front. She yells, "See that, Can't Get Right, I told you she would make something of herself. I can definitely pick 'em." "Yes Ma I know she's amazing," he replied. I'm not sure if he was being sarcastic or if this wasn't the first time Ms. Lana made that announcement and he was tired of hearing it.

As Ms. Lana showed me pictures of her beautiful granddaughter, I couldn't help but be distracted while Can't Get Right paced back and forth between his old room and the bathroom. He changed his shirt and I thought hmm that's interesting he still has clothes at his mother's apartment. "Can't Get Right, don't forget to fold up those clothes. I bought more stuff for my baby!" Ms. Lana yells loud and clear to him. When I heard fold up clothes I immediately flashed back to when I first moved in with Diablo. I noticed that once a week he would take my clothes out of the hamper and only put his dirty clothes in the laundry bag. When I finally asked what was going on, he told me his mother was doing laundry and had asked if he had anything that needed washing, but he didn't want her to see my things. I could not believe that this 25-year-old man had his mom washing his dirty undies. What the hell? So here's how I put a stop to it. Momma came knocking on the door to drop off his load. I kindly opened the door and pointed to the floor where she could drop the bag of laundry. With the sweetest smile I said, "Thank you so much for doing his laundry. Now when he goes to do mine he won't have so much. Have a good night." Let's just say my clothes were no longer removed from the hamper, and that was the end of Momma's laundry service as far as I knew. So the second red flag is waving and I'm so wrapped in my thoughts that I said, "You can't be serious." Ms. Lana responds, "Oh yes honey, my little princess gets gold stars every week. She is so smart." When I come back to reality, I say, "She sounds like such a gem!" Oh yeah I had a lot of questions for Can't Get Right. We were going to have a great talk.

As we are walking out the door Ms. Lana tells me to put her house, cell, and work number in my phone. Can't Get Right's cousin was getting married in Washington, DC and it would be great if I could come. She would give me all the details over the phone. She had not changed one bit. "As you can see, I'm not the only one that thinks you're the one that got away," Can't Get Right says to me. "Yep I can see that. Even Mr. Stevens gave you the thumbs up. I saw it in the lobby mirror," I say with a wink.

We walked and talked and it felt like old times. He told me about all of the degrees he earned, how much he loves his job, and how he wants to give his daughter the world. There was one question that I had to ask. "You live with your mother?" I'm not really sure how aggressively the question came out, but the nervous look on his face really gave it away. He said, "Yes, but I'm trying to move." He just had to get his finances in order. Now I understand people have set-backs. You're very blessed if your parents let you back in their home when something screws up in your life. That didn't bother me. Hell, it has happened to me. What concerned me was that he had never left. I feared he wasn't living up to his potential. The ambition was lacking and it was up to me, "Little Miss Fix It," to get that confidence back up. I believed in him and wanted to help him believe in himself.

A few weeks went by and I was all giddy. We spoke every day and I felt like Can't Get Right had the potential to get "it," know what I'm saying? Only thing that made me nervous was how anxious he was for me to meet his daughter. I love kids don't get me wrong, but it was a little soon and I was still trying to wrap my head around the fact that he had a kid with a stranger behind my back. Okay it didn't happen that way exactly, but man that was a hard pill to swallow.

I remember one night I was out with Nadia enjoying happy hour at PS 450 when Can't Get Right sent me a text asking if he could see me. I told him I was out with my girl and didn't know what time I would be done. He volunteered to meet me where I was and said he would sit by the bar until I was done. I was a little uneasy with that suggestion so I told him I would text when I was finished. I didn't want him waiting around like that and I would feel weird ignoring him. Nadia and I decided to call it a night around 10 o'clock. Can't Get Right told me he would meet me at the E 125th street train station. He wanted to take a stroll in the beautiful weather. I got out of the station and he was right there waiting as promised. I guess he knew if I didn't see him right away I would head home immediately.

There is absolutely nothing to do in that area at that time of night. So we were basically strolling with no destination. I had a long day and wasn't feeling this impromptu walk in the hood.

Here is the moment when I decided to pull back from Can't Get Right. I asked him to tell me more about his daughter's mother and he really didn't have anything positive to say other than she worked. After he finished complaining about her, he put his arm around me and said, "Man I would love to bump into her right now so she could see you." I was completely turned off. He may have thought he was giving a compliment, but I saw it as immature and petty. He could have kept that comment to himself. I told him I was tired and took a cab home. After that our conversations were far and few between.

One day while at work my buddy Sasha the receptionist calls to inform me that she had just left the mailroom and I had a huge package waiting for me. She could not stop laughing. My mind started racing; I had no idea who would send me anything. Vegas probably hated me by now and Diablo well, he knew better than to contact me. Sasha said, "I don't know. I'm not peeking in that big ass bag, but I do feel like there's a balloon in it." Now a lot of people knew of my annulment, but not everyone at work (I'm very private). "I'm bringing it down to you. I'm curious to know what it is."

She brings it to my desk. I open the bag and a huge heart balloon floats out. One side says "I miss you," the other side says "I love you." My face turned red immediately from embarrassment. I was flattered at the thought, but the balloon and what it said was overkill. "OMG, OMG, OMG who sent you that?" Sasha asks holding back laughter. I start looking for the card. It reads: "Sorry if I came on too strong. I'm happy to have you back in my life. I love you! Can't Get Right." "It's from my high school sweetheart," I say pissed. The balloon was attached to a huge Edible Arrangements® fruit basket. I love those, but I really hate balloons. This all happens while my very inquisitive co-worker comes in as if on cue and says, "Oh my goodness, well someone is trying to apologize to you huh?" I just smiled and shrugged my shoulders and stabbed the balloon with a pen. My co-worker Liza who I shared the news about my annulment with while on a business trip, was laughing hysterically and asked if she could have a chocolate covered pineapple. Sasha called dibs on the cantaloupe. While snacking on fruit, Liza and Sasha told me I should stop being so mean, and say thank you while expressing my love for Godiva® to see if he would send that next.

I called to say thank you and told him how surprised I was. He knew me well enough to know something was up, but I said I was fine. After all, I didn't want to come off as an ungrateful brat.

The more time I spent with Can't Get Right, the more I noticed he was in a time warp. Sulking over past mistakes he made with himself, with me, and with life. In a way, he had thrown himself a pity party. I really wanted to help him get out of his funk, but it became draining. I couldn't allow myself to be his main source of happiness. He needed to obtain happiness on his own first. Then I would have no problem adding to it. Our chatting everyday died down to once a week, once a month, then finally once every few months. In the time I was giving Can't Get Right some space to find his happy, I had an interesting meet cute with a Brooklyn native with a lot of charm and a big appetite for bagels.

#

Chapter 3: BagelBoy Break

Every morning I had a routine. Once I got off the train I would head to the bagel shop next door to buy breakfast. I ordered an egg and cheese sandwich on an everything bagel and then I would grab a yogurt. Once I got my breakfast, I would run across the street to get to work. This particular morning was a little different. I go inside and make my usual order and there was a cute, clean cut, 6ft tall guy near the register checking me out. I pretended not to notice. He gets a little closer to me and says, "Good morning beautiful." Immediately I thought well that was an original line...NOT. "Good morning," I say with a half-smile. I grab my yogurt and head to the register. We arrive at the counter at the same time. The cashier asked if there was anything else he wanted and he says, "Yeah let me get another lottery scratch off, this bagel I have here, and her breakfast." My ears perked up. "Who me? Wow, thank you so much." My first thought was, "he's getting better." My second thought was, "wow, a gentleman that's refreshing." My third thought was, "I should have ordered the flipping French toast." Damn!

We go outside and of course do the quick run-down of questions. Do you work around here? What's your name? Do you come here often? He was certainly very charming. He was a little huskier than what I was used to, but he told me when he stopped playing basketball he started gaining weight around the mid-section. He didn't have his phone with him, so he gave me his number and requested that he receive a text from me by the time he got to his desk. I said okay. I was letting him hold me hostage until he trusted I would text him. "Don't be a liar, it's unattractive," he yells as I walk away. I giggle and head to the office, free breakfast in tow, already debating whether or not to text him. I didn't want to seem like an eager beaver, but I did promise. Plus I'm an adult and put my foot down about not playing mind games. Decision made I'm texting.

Me: *Thanks again for the breakfast. That was really nice of you.*

Immediately I see the sent message turn blue. Any iPhone user knows that's major points for BagelBoy.

BagelBoy: *My pleasure beautiful with those eyes and that smile it was only right.*

This guy was really laying it on thick. I had to be careful with this one; I could tell already. We go back and forth all day texting and agree that we should meet after work for a happy hour drink. Cocktails were a hit. We laughed, shared stories about our families, and even discovered we knew a few of the same people. The world is so small sometimes.

Time goes on and our communication in the evening was minimal. We both had a second job, but did our best to make time for each other. Our after work cocktails became a regular thing. A little too regular; sometimes I just ordered water or juice. I can't drink every day. I'm already single, I can't be an alcoholic too. I met his co-workers and they all vouched that he was a good guy and thought we looked great together.

Smitten, I call my friend Victoria and tell her all about my new interest BagelBoy. Immediately she hits me with the 20 questions. "Does he have kids? How long has he been working across the street? What part of Connecticut does he live in? Does he own his home? Does he live alone? What's his 5 year plan? Did he graduate from college? Does he have a car? Does he have social media?" "My goodness woman, you've asked me everything but his blood type," I say laughing. "Ha girl, you crazy, but do you know it? I read somewhere people with type O are flexible and adopt easily to change." I originally went to the kitchen to make some tea, but knowing my friend I knew I would be in for an interesting conversation about this potential love interest of mine. I opted for a big Olivia Pope glass of Cabernet Sauvignon. After a gulp of wine and a deep breath I said, "Detective Vic, get to it. I want to know if he sneezed last night." She replied with a peppy, "I'm on it!" That's when the investigation of BagelBoy began. We went on to talk about shows we were watching, career moves we would like to make, and whether or not I should make brownies that weekend when I got another call. It was Can't Get Right. "Oh shit, it's Can't Get Right," I say all panicked, fixing my hair as if he could see me. "What the hell does he want?" Victoria asks with an attitude. "I don't know, but I have to call you back this should be good. Toodles noodles!" I say.

I click over and begin laughing like I'm having the time of my life. "Ha, I love this movie. Hello?" I say laughing. "Hey you it's been a long time. Sounds like you're having fun. Am I interrupting?" he asks laughing. "Can't Get Right? Oh wow! Hey no, not at all just watching *Bridesmaids*. I love this movie. Have you seen it? I can't believe she takes a poop in the middle of the street in her wedding dress! I'm doing great. How are you? How's the family?" I ask, taking a sip of wine. I was rambling and had no idea why I was slightly nervous. "No I haven't seen it. I was wondering if maybe we can do a happy hour tomorrow after my girls' basketball game. I know a great Mexican restaurant that makes really good margaritas. They're cheap, but you won't get a headache I promise," he says. I had an event the next day from 6am-4pm. I wasn't sure if I could handle hanging out after such a long day, but I figured why not, it's been a long time. Let's see what the man has been up to. "Okay sure I'll try to make the game, but if I miss it I can definitely make the Mexican happy hour," I say.

Now I have to find something to wear that is corporate event appropriate, but happy hour friendly. Sounds simple enough, but I struggled with it. It could have been the wine making this outfit decision a lot more difficult than it needed to be. I gave up and went to bed. I work well under pressure so I figured the outfit would come together while I'm rushing in the morning.

After a long day of dealing with registrants and hotel personnel I was exhausted. I wore a black and white stripped fit and flare dress. It showed a little too much cleavage, but nothing a cardigan and a string of pearls couldn't tone down. I wanted to continue to wear my heels, but I knew with Can't Get Right I would be doing a lot of walking and I needed to be comfortable. With my ballet flats on and my stilettos in my bag I was now ready to walk anywhere. I was on my way to his basketball game when I got a text from Victoria. She's got the scoop. Deep breath here we go.

Victoria: *Hey Chica, how was the event?*

Me: *Hey doll. Saw some cool presentations. Everything else was the same as every year. What's up?*

Victoria: *Nothing just heading over to my mom's to pick up the kids. Are you on your way to meet Can't Get Right? What did you wear? Are you with him now?*

Me: *No I'm on my way. I wore a dress. What did you find out?*

Victoria: *Which dress? Are you covering the girls?*

Me: *VICTORIA!!! I don't have a lot of time. I need you to focus and give me the scoop on BagelBoy.*

Victoria: *Alright! Alright! You know you're a little miss grumpy pants when you're sleepy. Anyhoo, he has a Facebook. I didn't know he coaches basketball in his spare time. He's got the most adorable nephew.*

Me: *Okay, okay this is all good stuff.*

Victoria: *Yeah he's a pretty good guy. I'm sure his girlfriend thinks so. His status says in a relationship. He's about to have a 1yr anniversary.*

Me: *Shut the Front Door! Are you fucking kidding me? That lying sack of…Oh hey, I'll text you later. I just arrived at the gym.*

Victoria: *Oh okay is it clean?*

Me: *Bye!*

Unbelievable! I knew BagelBoy was too good to be true.
I'll deal with him later. "Hi where is the basketball game?" I
asked a random. I knew I would miss the game on account that I
wasn't rushing to get there. I thought the little effort I put to
show up would be enough considering the long day I had and
this breaking news on BagelBoy. Ugh, he's such a creep.
"Upstairs!" the random replied. This rec center was really nice.
It's clean and bright and extremely inviting. Note to self: My
future kid could play basketball here. I turn to see a winding
staircase and immediately my body won't let me move until I
locate an elevator. I get on the elevator and press 2. The doors
open and there he is. Kids were pulling on him while he's talking
to one of the teenagers.

"Hello," I say, tired and confused as to why the gym is
empty. "Hey. Wow you look amazing. Wow! Yeah the game is
over. My girls lost so we're going to head out," he says sounding
disappointed. He kept a smiling face for the kids I suppose. I
said, "Oh wow okay so should I meet you downstairs now? Are
you ready?" I couldn't sound more unbothered about the fact
that his team lost. Maybe I was a dick as Vegas so eloquently
stated. I wasn't interested in seeing a game at all. Ah who cares?
Bring on the margaritas. I need one. As I sit downstairs waiting I
notice a group of teenage girls looking at me. I smile and of
course get a blank stare back. I'm not a fan of teenagers honestly.
You can't tell them anything and they think they know
everything. I go back to checking emails on my phone. Can't Get

Right comes running down the stairs and says, "You ready?" I stand up and said "Yeah!" at the same time as the 4 teenagers who were just giving me the ice stare. (Are you fucking kidding me?) "Let's go!" he says all enthusiastic and we all walk out together: me, him, and his basketball team.

He introduces me outside and that's when I get some smiles. Apparently he gave the girls a debriefing on how we knew each other. They were actually really sweet young ladies. He tells me he wants to walk with them to make sure they reach the train okay. I understand and I think it's very sweet, but where the hell is the train and where the hell is this restaurant? We've been walking too many blocks. "Here we are!" he says as we approach the restaurant door. I'm assuming the train is another block or so. He opens the door and in goes the team. What the hell is going on? How old are they? What is happening here? I came for happy hour with him not a team "after the game we lost, but that's okay" celebration. "You're bringing the kiddies to happy hour?" I whisper to him. "Ha oh no silly they're not drinking. They're too young. I wanted to feed them; it's a little tradition. After they eat it'll be just me and you," he says smiling. Well that's just fucking "Great!" I say out loud, well at least I think "great" is all I said out loud. He gives me a funny look. I really need to work on my outbursts.

So the waitress comes and hands out waters and menus. She asked if we wanted anything to drink and I say "What's your strongest alcoholic beverage?" I felt all eyes on me so I added a giggle. She suggested a margarita so that's exactly what I went with. The girls had never eaten at a Mexican restaurant before so I quickly explained the difference between burritos and enchiladas. They all ended up ordering burritos. They told me how coach helped build their confidence and they enjoyed playing and it made me understand why he loves his job. As he chugged his mini Coronas I could tell that although he was laughing and smiling there was the look of stress in his eyes. After my second margarita I said, "Are you okay?" He says, "Yeah of course. I'm with you." AWW, still a little charmer I see. I had to go to the restroom to text my friends that I was feeling better and there was no need to send the emergency escape text. As I get up to go to the restroom the waitress comes and brings the bill and I excuse myself. The last time I went out with Can't Get Right he patted his pockets a dozen times and just had enough to cover the bill. I had to leave the tip. He left his wallet in his bag in the trunk of my car. Well, that's what he told me. While in the restroom, I immediately send a text to Naomi.

Me: *Sooo as I'm getting up to go the restroom the waitress was bringing the bill. Oh and BagelBoy has a girlfriend.*

Naomi: *Ah shit here we go. Wait a what? Hey did you wear comfortable shoes?*

Me: *Yeah I put my ballet flats on why?*

Naomi: *Well at least you'll be comfortable when it's time to wash dishes LOL death to BagelBoy btw.*

Me: *No don't say that. I'm not washing shit. I'll pay my part and go the hell home you know me. Wait till I see BagelBoy in the morning.*

Naomi: *I can't stand you LOL get out the bathroom and tell me what happens, how many drinks did you have?*

Me: *Only 2 its happy hour it's like 2 for 1.*

Naomi: *2 LOL they're going to make you mop too.*

Me: *Goodbye*

Naomi: *Prepare for the pocket pat down! LOL.*

She's wrong that wouldn't happen again…right? Maybe that look of stress was about losing another game…right? Ugh! There's only one way to find out. I head out and everyone is still laughing and talking. I say "You ready? Let's get out of here." He says, "Yeah, just about to pay the bill." I watched this man keep his head down and count the same money 4 times. I wanted to tell him no matter how many times you fix the money it's the same amount. I reframed from being an asshole and I waited. He did not disappoint. As if on cue the pocket pat down began. Are you fucking kidding me right now? I'm not even drunk. This is some bullshit. In the sweetest voice I could produce I whisper, "Are you okay? What's wrong?" He looks up with the look of, I don't know, worry, maybe embarrassment, and says, "You have $20? I switched shorts and I guess I didn't take all my money out of the pockets." I was livid. How the hell do you invite me to happy hour and turn it into a feed the children brigade and not have enough to cover the bill? Am I wrong for feeling this way? He should have brought everyone pizza. I mean really who are you trying to impress? "Give me the cash I'll put the rest on my card," I manage to say without sounding utterly disgusted. I did not want to embarrass him in front of the girls so I smiled as I gritted my teeth signing the bill.

We leave and he wants to make sure the young ladies get on the train, so we walk all the way down into the subway and he says, "Everyone okay? Everyone have enough for the train fare?" Immediately my eyes pop out the sockets. Did he just ask them if they had train fare? And if they didn't, what were you going to do? You couldn't even cover the bill. OMG I'm going straight home. Can't Get Right had to get gone. I was so over these broke shenanigans. I pulled together a smile and said bye to the ladies and Can't Get Right decides to walk with me to my train.

He tells me more about his little princess and I shouted a few AWWs and wows, but I was over this entire evening and pretty much wanted to walk by myself. I wanted to figure out my attack on BagelBoy. Then Can't Get Right says, "I regret being a knucklehead when we were together back then. You turned out to be such a great person. I mean you always have been. You deserve a man that will have your dinner waiting for you when you get home and someone to massage your feet after a long day. I can do that for you." I can't lie I thought about how nice that would be, but only every once in a while. A man with no ambition could never make me dinner and rub my feet. He wouldn't be able to cook in my house let alone touch me. It was clear Can't Get Right lost his get-up-and-go, so I needed to get up and go. "Yeah that's sweet. I'm just going to take this train it's late. I'll text you. Have a good night," I say heading down the subway stairs. He looked disappointed, but it was clear the longer I stayed the more annoyed I would become. Besides that burrito was creeping up on me like nobody's business. I needed to rest so I could give BagelBoy a clear piece of my mind.

BagelBoy: *Good morning beautiful, looking forward to seeing you for breakfast.*

Well isn't that a nice way to wake up in the morning. Nothing like a text with a compliment from someone who wants to feed you.

Me: *Good morning you. I can't wait to see you too you lying sack of shit. Did you send your girlfriend the same message?*

No, no, no back space delete that, don't do it that way Shaunie. You need to see his eyes when you reveal your findings. Eyes don't lie.

Me: *Good morning you. I can't wait to see you too.*

I rush to get myself together for work. I wanted to look cute when I drop this news. I had my ammo ready. Social media is something. It will tell you everything you need to know without flat out asking. It's brilliant… well, in most cases. My train was delayed as usual, making me super late for work. So I missed my breakfast opportunity. He asked to meet up after work for drinks and I was not going to pass that up. I didn't care what day of the week it was I was drinking that Manhattan today. I practiced what I was going to say on Sasha.

Me: *What's up hot pocket how's your Hotty in Connecticut?*

Sasha: *Um too much. How about I saw your Facebook status asshole? Congratulations on your 1 year anniversary.*

Me: *I don't know I think that's revealing too much too soon. How about I just say so you have something you want to tell me? Keep in mind I already know so don't lie.*

Sasha: *Boys are dumb he'll never confess that way. I got it! Screen shot her picture and say who is she to you?*

Me: *Okay you totally just watched that Brandy video and no. It will come to me when I see him*

Sasha: *That song is awesome!*

5pm finally rolls around and I'm ready. Cat-eye makeup matched both eyelids. It's usually a hit or miss. You can either look like a sex kitten or an Egyptian ruler. I walked into the bar and spot him right away. He was laughing having a great time with his co-workers as usual. "Hey beautiful love your eyes. Here come sit," he says patting the seat next to him. I was not letting his charming ass distract me. I was a woman on a mission.

2 hours later and 4 Manhattans in, his co-workers finally leave and it's my time to strike. I really should have eaten more.

"Anything you want to tell me?" I ask. "Hmmm let's see, I really like you. You're smart, beautiful, and I really like your style," he says. "AWW really thank you. Wait no! No. That's not... No! Good wrong answer mister," I say slurring my words. "Who is she to you? Don't lie to meee," I sing slightly. He laughs and says, "Who is who? Somebody needs to lie down!" "Ugh Facebook you have an anniversary don't you?" I say, so frustrated. "What are you talking about? I'm a little buzzed you got to help me out," he says squinting. "Girlfriend! You have a girlfriend. It's on Facebook that you have a girlfriend," I say. "What? Look I am seeing someone, but she's not my girlfriend," he says with a straight face. "Oh really well does she know you're not her boyfriend? Your status says in a relationship," I say. Good job Shaunie that was loud a clear, I think to myself. The anger is building. "Who really keeps up with that? I haven't been on Facebook in months," he says all nonchalant. I get closer and look him dead in the eyeballs and say, "So you're sitting here telling me you don't have a girlfriend and you picked "in a relationship" as your status by default?" "Yes! Well no. She changed my status. I didn't know she did it at the time. I've been meaning to change it," he says, as his big brown eyes stay locked with mine. He was really trying to convince me. Either he thinks I'm an idiot or he thinks he's really that smooth. "Now can we move on from this nonsense? Give me a kiss," he says and puckers his lips grabbing me. I turned my face displaying an angry pout and the kiss lands on my ear. Gross! I stand up and grab my belongings. "I'm leaving. Text me when you want to tell the truth," I say with utter disgust. "Let me walk you to your train," he yells. "I'll be fine it's across the street," I yell back and I proceed to the door which oddly enough seems a lot further away after a few drinks. He grabs my arm and helps me up the stairs and walks me to my train anyway. I gave him a hug for his good deed, but he wasn't off the hook. I was pissed and determined to get to the bottom of this.

My alarm goes off in the morning and I hit snooze. I hit snooze 3 times. My head was pounding and I couldn't call out because I'd inflicted this pain on myself. So I put my big girl panties on and start to get ready for work when I hear my phone. It's his text tone. Ugh here we go. What lies do you want to tell me today BagelBoy?

BagelBoy: *Good morning beautiful. Be early today so we can sit and have breakfast together.*

Is he for real? This guy is still going. Ugh I really need to eat my head is pounding. No, no, no he can't win me over with French toast. Damn I want some French toast.

Me: *Good morning. I won't be able to make that. Enjoy your day.*

I chugged some water and left the house. It was sad knowing that I would eventually have to change my breakfast spot.

I arrive at work and Sasha calls me immediately. It's like she knew. I just sat at my desk. "Tell me everything. What did he say? Did he lie? Did he confess that lying bastard?" she says aggressively. I have to admit her excitement got me all amped up again. "No he didn't confess really. He said that's not his girlfriend and he hasn't updated his Facebook in months. I want to believe him, but the proof is right in my face," I say with a big sigh. "You deserve better. Clearly he's confused about what he wants. He's messy. OMG did you get breakfast? Was he there?" Sasha asks. "No I didn't and I'm starving and I have a headache and I really want some freaking French toast! He ruined everything!" I say whining. "You're so greedy. Go to the breakfast place next door. Cheer up doll. I have to answer these calls. People are so annoying. Toodles!" she says as she hangs up. Sasha was right. I did deserve better so I cut him off… well in my head I did.

I arrived at Job2 early so I decided to kill some time and see what nonsense I could laugh at on Instagram. There he was, the first picture on my timeline, in his fitted suit and the shirt I went with him to pick up from Bloomingdales. I forgot he was going to Atlantic City for the weekend. Wait who took the picture? I tried to zoom in and damn it forgot you can't do that on Instagram. Now I've liked the picture. I can't take it back he'll know. Ugh why was this happening? And of course as if on cue there goes his text tone.

BagelBoy: *Hey beautiful! I've been thinking about you. How does the suit look?*

Me: *I'm working can't talk now.*

BagelBoy: *Okay have a good night. See you Monday?*

I didn't reply. We're not friends. He doesn't deserve a reply. Damn it. How is it time to clock in already? Well, it's time to make the donuts. As I'm putting merchandise on the shelf, I'm thinking to myself, who the hell took that picture? Was it the girlfriend? Why do I even care? This is so stupid. He's a liar that looks really good in a suit and smells like fresh soap, expensive cologne and just amazing. "Shaunie, Shaunie it's time to go to lunch. Are you okay?" my partner says to me. Poor thing I must have been ignoring him all evening. "What? Yes I'm okay. Did I look out of it or something? Don't answer that." I quickly go downstairs to grab my car keys. I needed to go to my car and relax for my 45 minute break. Of course I get in my car and do what? Yeah you guessed it, opened that Instagram. Scrolling,

scrolling, scrolling and boom there it is. This asshole posts a picture of him and her with the caption: Just us. Are you fucking kidding me? So I did what any 21st century petty princess would do in this situation. I liked the picture to let him know I saw it and then I took a screen shot and sent it to Robyn, Naomi and Victoria. The first responder was Victoria. She was up feeding the baby.

Victoria: *EWW that's the girl from Facebook. Are they celebrating their anniversary?*

Me: *You know I really didn't even think of that. He's wearing the shirt and with her. WOW!*

Victoria: *You should send him the picture and tell him what part of your butt to kiss.*

Me: *No I'll get him. I really wanted to give him the benefit of the doubt.*

Victoria: *Some people don't deserve*

Me: *Deserve what?*

Victoria: *Sorry, baby burped and went exorcist on me. Spit up everywhere. I'll text you in the morning.*

She was right just like Sasha was right. He didn't deserve anything I had to offer. I'm telling him about himself tomorrow. He needs to know he cannot contact me anymore. And I am no longer following you on Instagram mister. Bad Boy take that. Can't stop, won't stop. I had to do my little Diddy dance for putting my foot down.

Monday finally arrives and I'm ready. I texted him first and said good morning sunshine! Are you free for lunch today? He took the bait. 12:30pm he was getting a piece of my mind and I was certainly telling him what part of my ass to kiss. Before leaving work to meet him I head to the ladies room. I had to make sure I was well put together. You can't take anyone seriously with eye boogers or dry elbows.

As I walk toward his job I start to get a little nervous. He's always dressed so cute in his business casual attire and I know he's going to ask for a hug and then I have no choice but to sniff him. It really is a vicious cycle. Well that cycle breaks today! He's going to feel the wrath of "Oh hello BagelBoy," I say as I smack right into him. I really need to pay more attention to my surroundings when I'm talking to myself. "Hey beautiful you look so focused, like you had something going on in that head of yours. You almost walked right past me," he says all charming with his arms out for a hug. I smacked them down. "No hugs for you. Cute picture! How was Atlantic City? Did she enjoy her anniversary trip?" I say with one eyebrow raised. My tone was perfectly petty. I just hope my resting bitch face matched. "Whoa, Whoa, Whoa so no hug seriously?" he says. My blank stare must have been serious because he just let it all out. "Okay we were both in Atlantic City, but she stayed with her friends and I stayed with mine. It was not an anniversary trip." "Bullshit! Don't you get tired of lying? Why can't you just be honest? Do you have a girlfriend? Is that your girlfriend?" I ask. Now I was focused. I couldn't care less how good he smelled.

"Yes!" he says, finally confessing. "Why did you lie? I'm a cool person right? Aren't I easy to talk to? What were you looking to gain?" I ask. I was on auto pilot at this point. I got no sleep from the night before and I wanted to get this over with. "I really like you. You're a total package. I couldn't let you get away. I want you to be my girlfriend," he says. "What? You already have a girlfriend," I say, sleepy and really confused at this point. "So!" he says, shrugging his shoulders. "What the hell do you mean 'so?'" I yell. "I want you to be my girlfriend too," he says innocently. "Girlfriend two as in number 2? Are your fucking kidding me?" I yell. "Hear me out. You can be my girlfriend too. Not number 2, but too as in also; like my Manhattan girlfriend." "Ha! You are sick. Look at me. 'Two is not a winner and 3 nobody remembers.'3 Lose my number BagelBoy," I say. As I walk away, I am proud of the Nelly lyrics I flawlessly delivered. I could not believe the audacity of this man to make such an absurd proposal. The balls on this dude were huge. "Where's your competitive spirit?" he yells. I threw up my middle finger and continued to walk away. It wasn't the lie that irritated me, it was the fact that he kept trying to insult my intelligence that pissed me off. Thank you God I didn't give him any. I would have caught a case. I needed comfort and immediately I wondered how Superman was doing. He always saves the day.

#

Chapter 4: Superman... The history of my Cuddy

Can someone tell me what the hell I have written on my forehead? Hey are you insecure, financially troubled, or a liar? Then go on and ask for my number. I love a challenge. I need a vacation where I can just lay out in the sun, clear my mind and relax. I could not get Superman out of my head. I really didn't want to text him because it had been a while since we last well… you know. Plus I had ended our escapades too many times before. We were practicing being platonic and, well so far so good. "No, no sorry this order is wrong. I asked for bacon. You know what? Forget it," I say to the man behind the counter. I started my diet today and forgot already. I hate this new breakfast spot. Tomorrow I'm totally going back to my original place whether I run into BagelBoy or not. It is one thing to lie about your relationship status, but it's a whole other thing to mess with someone's breakfast.

I take a deep breath and really contemplate texting Superman again. Our conversations were so generic these days. We were both really trying not to text each other perverted texts that would end up with a scheduled take down session. One little text couldn't hurt right? It's not like I was looking to start things up again. What's one more quickie for about 45 minutes to a weekend huh? We're both mature adults. How bad could it be?

You know what, no I'm not. I'm stronger than this. I decided to find out what Naomi was doing instead so I texted her.

Me: *Hey pop tart good morning.*

Naomi: *Hey smitten kitten. Not much going on. LeBoyfriend is being a real pain in my ass and I'm hungry.*

Me: *LOL he's always a pain in your ass and you're always hungry. Oh and the kitten died.*

Naomi: *I can't stand you. Who did it?*

I tell Naomi all about my last encounter with BagelBoy and how I'm on a dating hiatus. On cue as if she was reading my mind all morning, she texts.

Naomi: *So are you going to make Superman an offer?*

Me: *Heavens no! Why on earth would I do such a thing? I'm a lady I do declare... I'm texting him at lunch.*

Naomi: *High five that's my girl. You control the kitty not the other way around. When you're done you kick his ass out. None of that here's a snack shit.*

Me: *Oh please, I'm not cooking for him anymore. He's taken now remember. He's not even happy.*

(sigh)

Naomi: *Look I love you guys together. You were there first remember that. He's yours until you say he's not.*

Me: *LOL I was not there first...oh great, now my devil horns have popped out. Thanks a lot! I'm blaming you for all the trouble that may occur in advance.*

Naomi: *I'm team Shaun. LOL*

Now that I have the backing of one of my nearest and dearest friends, Operation: Trip to Krypton was underway. Of course he would text me at the very moment I make a decision about him.

Superman: *Hello*

How is it he always does that? It appears that whenever I tend to think of this man he always texts me. It's like we were connected somehow.

Me: *Good afternoon Friend.*

Superman: *Just checking in on a friend. How are you?*

Me: *I'm well thank you for asking. So listen I was thinking maybe if you're free sometime during the week maybe we can have a pizza and wine night, maybe watch a movie on Netflix?*

Superman: *YES. Does Tuesday work for you?*

Me: *Tuesday is perfect.*

As I do a little dance in my chair I can't help but wonder what the hell did I just do? I hope he doesn't think we are back on because we are most certainly not. Maybe he'll say something stupid between now and Tuesday and I can back out of this impulsive decision.

Superman: *I'll bring the pizza. I know the best pizza place in NYC.*

Me: *I'll be the judge of that.*

Superman: *If I'm right I get to pick the movie.*

Me: *I accept your challenge good man.*

Damn he's good. I'm sure he knows exactly when to ask me my thoughts on his pizza. Mmm, mmm, mmm he's not slick. If we can make it through the evening without any extra-curricular activities then we have mastered self-control and can keep this platonic friendship going. If not, well then we can never be alone together. It's just that simple.

Let me give a little background story on this superhero. Superman and I used to flirt with each other back when I worked part time at the gym. We started working there at the same time. He was a new trainer and we bonded immediately being the new kids on the block. Our work schedules were the same all the time. We became friends very fast. He was a Hotel Manager full-time so yes, the man knew how to put a suit together. He hands-down has the most amazing shoulders I've ever seen. I was never really sure about his marital status because we talked about so many other things. I figured if it was major like a girlfriend or a wife it would have come up at some point very early on. We were just work friends anyway. He knew I had Vegas and so I never pressed the issue. He did have a 2-year-old son. Not something I was thrilled about, but I was considering being exclusive with Vegas at the time so it didn't matter. Superman got the second job because he wanted to move and the money he made working at the gym would help him do that a lot quicker. I was in the same boat minus the kid. I wanted to move out of my grandmother's apartment quickly back then. Sometimes a second job is a quick fix, but it is not a long term solution. Having multiple sources of income is very important. There is a smarter way to accomplish that without putting the physical strain on your body. You just have to challenge your brain more. One thing I learned is it's hard to enjoy the fruits of your labor when all you do is labor.

I remember the time I had a work event coming up and I decided to invite Superman and his friend. There would be plenty of food and wine at the event so he would certainly have a great time. I was really starting to like this guy and besides, he needed to see me all dressed up and not in the usual drab gym t-shirt we had to wear for work. I wore a fitted black leather dress. Go hard or go home I always say.

Superman and I had been emailing back and forth the morning of the event. In our minds, emails were innocent and platonic. I was really excited to see him later and I was determined to get the scoop on his relationship with his child's mother. I knew I was playing with fire, but I was interested in him and I wanted him to know. I hired my friend Sabina to help out with registration and told her all about Superman. She assured me she would be my lookout for when he arrived so I could of course make a grand entrance. He already told me he would be running late so I kept calm and handled my onsite event duties.

Sabina: *Um there are two really tall guys in line to enter the ballroom. They look like athletes. Is one of them him?*

Me: *I don't know I can't see I'm not on your floor.*

Sabina: *Well get your hot ass up here. They are cute so whether it's him or not, you need to meet them and introduce me.*

Me: *I can't right now the vendors all arrived at the same time. Check-in is crazy.*

Sabina: *Phuck those vendors your future husband is here.*

Me: *OMG your language young lady.*

Sabina: *What I used the PH?*

Me: *LOL coming up.*

I finished my task and headed up about 15 minutes later. I checked my email and saw Superman had emailed me his phone number (email took too long); he wanted me to text him when I was around. I told Sabina and she told me in order to get him out the room I should text him, "Bring your fine ass out here and bring your friend for my friend." I said okay and texted.

Me: *Hey Superman. Thank you for coming. I should run into you soon.*

Superman: *I'm having a great time. Thank you for inviting me. My friend is making friends with all the vendors.*

Me: *LOL Social I like that.*

Superman: *Where are you? I'll come to you.*

Me: *Okay. I'm by the registration area.*

"OMG, he's coming. How do I look?" I whisper to Sabina. "You look scrumptious. See I told you that text would work," she said proudly. I gave her a high five and fluffed up my hair. I saw him coming out so I decided to "bump into him." Sabina and I walk over laughing, clearly having a great time and boom. "There you are. Hey Superman! Hello Superman's friend!" I say. "Hi nice to meet you, I'm Gerard," his friend says with a firm hand shake. "This is a great event thank you for inviting us," Gerard says. "Hi I'm Sabina nice to meet you Gerard. Look at all those business cards pouring out of your pocket. Wow that's a good handshake," Sabina says. Then she turns to me and says, "I'm going back to work. It was nice meeting you both," she says to the guys as she walks away. I'm smiling at her giving her the "what the hell" stare down. As she walks away backwards, she gives me the "Beyoncé put a ring on it" wave as I realized she had lost interest because Gerard had a wedding band on. I totally understood. Superman's fingers were bare hallelujah.

As I'm talking to Gerard, I can feel Superman's eyes giving me a complete body scan. "You look amazing," Superman says with the ultimate creep look in his eyes. He was either a little tipsy, or being a pervert, or a little combination of both. "Thank you," I reply sweetly. "You look very handsome yourself." He said thank you, offering the most humble hand to chest gesture. He was such a clown. "So did you fellas meet some interesting people?" I ask, and right away Gerard jumps on the answer. "I don't know how many times people asked us if we were athletes and what team we played for. I told the first few no I'm a business man not a pro athlete." I could tell he was slightly offended as he continued. "Just because they see a black man that's 6'6" does not mean he plays professional sports. I get there aren't too many of us here at the event, but to assume that's my profession instead of just asking is wrong." "Well you could have used it to your advantage, they could have invited you to one of their private events, and you could be drinking all night for free," I reply jokingly. "You are funny. That's what Superman said," Gerard says laughing. Superman chimed in: "Yeah so after a few glasses I started to answer 'yes' to the athlete question. 'Why yes I am a pro athlete. I play for the Saints, but I'm mostly on the bench.'" We laughed hysterically. Gerard said Superman's clever response changed the experience for the rest of the night. That explained why he had so many business cards. The vendors wanted him to attend parties as their VIP. That event changed the dynamic of my friendship with Superman. It was clear we wanted to get closer, but I needed to verify some important details.

After my event, our communication became a little more intense. I mean we did upgrade from emailing to texting now. No more innocent sporadic emails. It was through text that he opened up about his relationship status. It turned out that Superman and his child's mother were in an "on-again off-again" relationship. He told me he had an "oops moment" (son) and was trying to make the best of it. He and the child's mother didn't see eye-to-eye on a lot of things. He made sure he saw his son 3-4 times a week and had him every other weekend. I admired his efforts to be in his son's life, but I was very bothered by the child's mother giving him such a hard time. Granted, I only knew his side of the story, but I knew I didn't want to get in too deep. A relationship with him would just be messy and I was kind of in a relationship myself so I needed to pull back. He had a good head on his shoulders; he was funny and was so handsome. I put him in my next lifetime box: if in another life our paths should ever cross we would be together for sure.

While at work Superman and I decided to take lunch together. He told me he was going to Canada to visit his favorite cousin. In my head, Canada would be the perfect place to see if my superhero could rescue me from my sex drought. Vegas was away and being so annoying. Plus we said we wouldn't make our exclusivity official until my annulment was final so technically I was a free agent. "I love road trips. How long is the ride? I've never been to Canada before!" I said, sounding overzealous. "I'm going in a couple of weeks. It's like an 8 hour drive. Are you trying to go?" he asked, as his devil horns start to rise from his head. He's such a pervert and I just love it. At this point we have never kissed or got cheap feels. Our hugs did change. They got longer and tighter each time. "Yeah if you want the company I mean I don't want to impose, but I'm super fun on road trips," I say enthusiastically. I think to myself, down girl what the hell is wrong with you? "Of course I would love your company. Are you packing pajamas?" he asks jokingly. "I usually sleep naked, but for this trip I will make the exception and pack accordingly," I say with a devilish smirk. It must have caught him off guard because he almost choked on his sandwich. After a huge gulp of Gatorade he says, "By all means pack what you feel the most comfortable in."

I could not believe I was going on a road trip to Canada, let alone with Superman. This would be our first time alone and for an entire weekend. I suggested we take my car just in case he's a jerk. This way I can leave his ass in Canada and that on-again off-again child's mother of his can pick him up. What the hell was I going to pack? Pajama shorts of course, but I'm not packing lingerie, that would be too presumptuous. So I decided to text my trusty advisors.

Naomi: *Why are you packing PJs? You've made it clear you sleep naked.*

Me: *Because I already invited myself on the trip. I'm not trying to be the aggressor here.*

Robyn: *Don't feel that way. In life you have to go after what you want. Wear boy shorts and a tank.*

Naomi: *That's cute I like that. Buy a set, a lace set in his favorite color.*

Me: *I have hello kitty shorts. They're sexy with that innocent feel to it.*

Robyn: *Oh yeah go ahead and he'll say hello to your kitty alright.*

Me: *LOL I'll pack a few PJs and see how the evening goes. That will determine what I whip out.*

Naomi: *Smart girl and throw some thongs in there and edible panties.*

Me: *NAOMI!!!!*

Naomi: *What, too much? You're right they don't taste good anyway.*

Robyn: *LOL Dare I ask Naomi. How do you know that?*

Naomi: *LeBoyfriend said they taste horrible. I didn't believe him so I snatched a piece off and well those shits are gross.*

Me: *LOL I'm done. I'm going shopping tomorrow for ladylike PJs.*

Robyn: *Are you sure your friendship can handle this? You're not a casual sex kind of girl. 99% of the time you're right back in a relationship.*

Naomi: *So true Robyn. You better man up and stand your ground. Enjoy the single life for awhile. Wait have you seen his mister? Can you tell if it's big or small? OMG what if he has a tiny pecker and tries to quick pump you all night? LOL*

Robyn: *LOL I was thinking about that, but didn't want to be negative.*

Me: *LOL seriously? He's 6'6" 230lbs with a size 14 shoe and huge hands. There is nothing small about that man I assure you.*

Naomi: *Okay smitten kitten. Time will tell. Pack a toy as back up.*

Me: *I don't have a toy.*

Robyn: *You might want to add that to your shopping list.*

As I write sex toy on my shopping list I start thinking to myself that maybe this is not a good idea. I'm not sure if I can handle just sex. What if it's great and I get all attached and he's like but you said it's just sex and I'm like yeah well I changed my mind you're my boyfriend now so spoil me. Aren't I allowed to say that? It's my right as an independent woman to lock down amazing penis whenever I'm ready, and the owner of this amazing penis has to oblige. And with that said I put the glass of wine down and went to bed.

I woke up the next day refreshed. I was a woman on a mission. After work I was going to meet up with Victoria and we were hitting the Village for my sex toy. She was so excited to get out of the house and escape mommy duty for a while she didn't care where we went. Since we're venturing out to the land of the naughty, I figured we could look for a kinky outfit as well. Victoria sent me pictures of sex toys all day. I had no idea if I would even use one let alone what kind and color.

Victoria: *So what about this one?*

Me: *I don't even know what that does.*

Victoria: *It's a penis ring. He wears it and it vibrates. It's not bad if you get a good one.*

Me: *How does it even go on? He's not going to put that on. It looks tight.*

Victoria: *No silly it stretches. Just put it on after he puts on the condom. Get really drunk and just go for it. That's how I do it.*

Me: *This is also how you end up with surprise babies.*

Victoria: *Shut up! I can't help it if my husband finds me irresistible.*

73

Me: Yeah and vice versa horn dog. You know too much about these toys. I'll see you at 5:30. Let's meet at a restaurant and then walk together to the Pink Pussy Cat. I don't want you to be late and I'm standing in front of it alone looking like a creep.

Victoria: LOL you won't look like a creep. You'll look like a woman of the 21st century taking control of her sexual needs.

Me: I don't want to look like anything. I want to get in and get out.

Victoria: That's what he said LOL.

Me: Bye

Victoria had a point. Why should I be shy about taking care of my sexual desires? After all I'm a grown woman. I could do what I want when I want. I'll simply walk in and with oodles of confidence say, "Hi yes hello, which aisle are the penis rings?" and then make my purchase and leave. Let's be honest, who would be in there to judge right? Certainly not the employees, they applied to work there. Not the owner. They ordered all the freak stuff in there. And for damn sure not the other customers; we are all in here shopping discretely together. Let the freak flag fly! Oh yay! I did bring my sunglasses. I'm totally putting those on.

The day dragged and all I could think about was being in Canada with this extremely attractive man with a sex toy in my bag. How was I even going to whip it out? Should I notify him at dinner that hey if the sex is boring I have a back-up plan to spice things up? This is too much. Just as I complete my thought Superman texts me. It was as if I sent out some sort of signal.

Superman: Good afternoon friend!

Me: Good afternoon sir. How's your day going?

Superman: *It's going. Boss isn't here yet. He's more annoying when he's not in the office.*

I typed, "Buying a sex toy after work today. How do you feel about penis rings?" and deleted it immediately.

Me: *LOL I know oh too well how that goes. Are you ready for next week?*

Superman: *Of course. What kind of alcohol do you like?*

Me: *Oh it's that kind of party? Vodka!*

Superman: *Me too. I'll buy it for the trip and get the juice. It can be whatever kind of party you want. We can have a pajama jammy jam.*

Me: *What do you know about House Party? That's one of my favorite movies.*

Superman: *Oh come on everyone knows Kid 'N Play.*

Me: *I may have to test your movie knowledge skills in Canada.*

Superman: *Hope that's not the only skills you test out.*

Me: *LOL oh my!*

Okay clearly this was a man with an agenda and I was ready to partake in the foolery. Skills? Ha this guy. Did he really say skills? I had to read that text again. He was going to make me fall in love. I just knew it. Why play with fire? Why go somewhere with a guy who can't maintain a consistent relationship status? What am I doing? The thoughts continued to run through my head and out of nowhere I had a sudden overwhelming feeling of guilt. I started to feel our trip was wrong and that we should cancel. What about the child's mother? Was their relationship "off" for good this go round? What about the sex toy? There was no way I could insult this man by whipping out a penis ring. I took a deep breath and decided to let the chips fall where they may. It would be an experience regardless. My thoughts were all over the place. One minute I was feeling guilty, the next I was thinking of ways to remove the man's clothes. The only thing I knew for sure was that I wanted to spend time with him alone. I needed to know if these butterflies I felt were because we could possibly have something real or if it was just infatuation.

I hate going to the Village. Every time I come out of the subway station there, my sense of direction is all out of whack. I always need a landmark. Where the hell is that Chase bank? Oh there it is. Damn that's far. I thought to myself. Clearly I came out the wrong exit. I whip out my phone and Google mapped directions. As I get a little closer I see Victoria waving me down in front of the Pink Pussy Cat. I feel my face turn hot and red. I'm so embarrassed that my friend is signaling me to come into a sex shop. I darted across that street like Tina Turner braving that 6 lane highway.

"Hey girl come on let's go!" I say to Victoria as we dive into freak world.

"Hi ladies welcome! How can I assist you today?" the pleasant saleswoman says. "She needs a penis ring," Victoria says loud and clear. "Um NO, no I don't! I don't need anything, we're just looking," I say in a desperate attempt to remain un-judged. Victoria and I go up and down each crowded aisle. After pushing every button to make something vibrate, light up, or pulse, and saying "EWW" like grossed-out school kids, I finally picked a clear penis ring with 7 speeds. I felt good about my purchase although I was unsure if I would use it. One thing I knew for sure. It was going to Canada!

The time had finally arrived and I was on my way to meet Superman. I wore my hair big and curly because he loved it, a white tee-shirt very boob friendly, a pencil denim skirt, and fun converse sneakers. I was casual, but giving a little something without trying too hard. He walked over to the car looking amazing in his tee-shirt, cargos, and shades I don't know what it is about a good looking man with a fresh haircut, but it drives me crazy. And if the man smells good, Jesus take the wheel. I'm sure you could see the hearts in my eyes. I decided to wait until he got closer to the car before I got out. He was driving so I needed to switch to the passenger seat. Could I have just slid over to the other seat Of course I could have, but let's be real, where's the fun in that. Besides, I wanted a hug and I wanted to sniff his neck. "Well, well, well good morning curly hair girl with the light eyes!" he says. "Good morning handsome! Are you ready to get this show on the road?" I ask blushing. "Yes absolutely!"

We had a great time from the 8 hour car ride, to visiting his cousin briefly, to having dinner over-looking Lake Ontario, to holding hands just walking the streets of Toronto. We were so drunk when we got back to our hotel room. We had an intense make-out session, but my guilty conscience would not let me sleep with this man. I thought about Vegas, I thought about his child's mother, and the fact that he and I worked together. It would just be messy. He was buck naked with just his socks on, ready to take me down, but he understood I was not having any of that. We were friends first; so he placed the gold wrapper on the night stand and told me it would be there just in case I changed my mind. He checked a few times to see if I was ready to use it, but I said no. Nothing was going down. He was a perfect gentleman.

When I woke up the next morning I was curled up at the end of the bed. He was at the top of the bed tucked under the covers sleeping very stiff with his arms folded. I went to the top of the bed to get under the covers with him and he put his arm around me so I could rest in his nook. Next life time is all I kept thinking to myself. On the drive back I had to confess something to him. After all we were friends. I thought it was only right that I should be honest. "Superman, I just want to say thank you for being a perfect gentleman. Honestly it made me like you even more," I said. "Hey listen we didn't come here for that. I mean don't get me wrong I wanted that. I wanted all of that, but it's cool. I have a lot of respect for you," he says as he grabs my thigh. "That means a lot coming from you. I have a secret. Are you ready?" I ask. "Um are you sure you want to share this while I'm driving?" "It's nothing crazy silly, but you should know that if you tried to sleep with me this morning, I'm 100% sure you would have succeeded," I say nodding my head yes. "ARE YOU FUCKING KIDDING ME? We're turning around. WHAT? You are something else young lady," he said, shaking his head with his hands tightly on 10 and 2 of the steering wheel. "Oh and I bought a sex toy."

Superman didn't get the panties until after Vegas and I were broken up. We had both moved on from the gym, but we still kept in contact. It was like we became obsessed with one another. He brought things out of me no one did. There was always a sense of comfort with him. Our bodies were in sync almost as if we were sex soul mates. Honestly, you could even drop the sex and just keep the soul mates. The mental was always present. I think that's what made the physical even more intense. We were like best friends that had sex occasionally. It wasn't until he got engaged that I had to move on. Either we were going to just be friends or nothing at all. We learned so much about each other over the years. We were very close. It would not be easy to just walk away, but let's face it, I can't live on Krypton forever.

My intercom rang and all of sudden my nerves took over my body. I did a quick mirror check to make sure I was well put together. Hair big and fluffy, red lips glossy, white pants fitted, okay just friends on 3. 1, 2, 3. I give myself a high five and open the door. "Hello Superman!" I say as innocently as possible. The pizza box hits the floor and I get carried to my bedroom. I guess we can go back to being platonic tomorrow.

#

Chapter 5: Adventures with StickyFingers

I wake up the next morning bright eyed and bushy tailed, singing in the shower like I was performing a concert. I'm even up early enough to make my own breakfast. Look at me on time, saving money, and "adulting" this beautiful sunny morning. I grab my phone for the routine Instagram scroll and see if I missed anything hilarious. When I look at the screen I see all these texts, all from this morning. What the hell?

Can't Get Right: *Good morning Gorgeous. Haven't heard from you in a while. You stay blessed.*

I will. Delete!

Vegas: *Hey beautiful I'm in town this weekend lets meet up.*

Never again in this lifetime. Delete!

BagelBoy: *Good morning sexy. You know you hungry. Meet me for some French toast.*

Damn that sounds good, but not with you. Delete!

Mom: *Call me when you get to work.*

Why wouldn't she just call my work phone at 9:30 as usual? She must have gossip.

Superman: *Morning!*

Yessssss now we're talking.

Me: *Good morning Superman. Hope you slept well.*

Superman: *I did, very well. I'm very relaxed.*

Me: *Your pizza was delicious.*

Superman: *You're wine made it better.*

Me: *Are we still talking about dinner?*

Superman: *I don't know, but I like it LOL*

Me: *Clown LOL. Have a great day. I'm going to be on time for work today. I got to go.*

Superman: *Thank you. You have a great day as well sunshine.*

I love when he uses my words. He's so amazing. I don't know if the stars were aligned or if I was just floating on air from the cuddy I got last night, but my commute was delay free. I got to work before my boss and was able to get some work done with no interruptions. What a great morning! I made sure I called my mother before she called me and asked if I saw her text. "Good morning Mother!" I say with a great British accent. "Good morning daughter!" she replies. "We have to talk about this cruise. Your brother said he can drop us off at the airport in your car so tell him what time to pick you up." "Wait what? What time to pick me up? Pick me up in my car? Okay you're confusing things already. I will talk to him," I say slightly confused as to how my car got involved. "Fine and call your Aunt. She wants to wear red for the Captains Dinner. Oh and she said we should pack something all white because there will be an all-white party on the deck," Mom says. "Okay." I say nonchalantly. "Okay? It's that easy? You have something red and something all white? You two make me sick. So I'm the only one that has to go shopping? I hate shopping. Now I have to find a red dress?" she complains. "Um excuse me young lady. You have 2 weeks, which in my opinion is more than enough time considering you work right across the street from the discount retail giant Century 21. Now put your big girl panties on and while you're on your lunch break hit those racks," I say in my coach voice. "That's a very nasty attitude you have. I don't want to talk to you goodbye," she says laughing. "I love you too pumpkin byeeee!" I sing.

I check my calendar and it appears both my girls have a birthday coming up. The timing could not be more perfect. Restaurant week was coming up as well. What better way to celebrate my two favorite Leos than by having yummy food and strong drinks. Note to self: Call Naomi and Victoria later to find out birthday plans.

Work was slow. A lot of people go on vacation in August so you really can't get too much done until after Labor Day. So I decided to do a little online browsing. I was going on my first cruise in a couple of weeks. We were celebrating my aunt's 50th birthday and we decided to kick things off in New Orleans and take the cruise ship from there. Our ports were Honduras, Belize, and Cozumel. Perhaps I would meet some tall dark and handsome island man who had tons of money and wanted to spoil me rotten and pamper me. Or maybe on the boat there would be a single good looking guy on vacation with his family and we'd meet and fall in love on the deck. The possibilities were endless and that's why I need to purchase these sandals right now. Shoes say a lot about a person. These said "rich island man take me away."

Naomi and Victoria decided they wanted to go to Sofritos for their birthday celebration dinner. They have the best empanadas and delicious sangria. This was going to be a great night. We get to the restaurant and it is crowded. Apparently everyone was celebrating something that night. I'm so happy I made reservations. "Hey ladies, excuse me beautiful ladies let me take your picture. We put them on the website to showcase our night life," the pushy photographer said. "Okay let's do it. We're celebrating birthdays tonight Ayyyyee!" Victoria says overly-excited. "We really need to get you out the house more," Naomi says. "Mind you this is before drinks," I tease. "Whatever, smile for the man so we can go sit down. I'm hungry," Victoria says. We take our picture and of course Naomi makes us take it twice because we can't take the chance of us looking crazy on the Internet. We get to our table and all you hear are the waiters singing happy birthday in Spanish. Of course I'm singing along as I pull out my chair. I look up and Naomi and Victoria are both giving me the look of death. "Fine I won't tell them it's your birthdays, party poopers," I say slightly disappointed. We order our food and here comes the pitcher of sangria. As Victoria begins to pour she says "Soooo are we going to pretend like you and Superman are not on again?" Naomi chimes in. "Yeah how many times have you seen him since your wine and pizza night?" "Oh okay I see how this night is going to go. It's the Interrogation Celebration I see. Well if you must know we only saw each other the one time thank you. We had a moment of weakness. We're fine now," I say with the utmost confidence. I don't know if I was trying to convince them or myself. "So you're telling me right now if that man said hey girl I want to make you walk funny, you would be like oh no thank you Superman I enjoy my walk just the way it is?" Victoria asks sarcastically. "First of all he wouldn't say that. Second of all, no one would say any of that EVER. Did you have a nap today?" I ask in a motherly tone. And like a big kid Victoria sulks her shoulders, lowers her eyes and says, "No!"

Third pitcher of sangria in and we are all singing happy birthday in Spanish. Our waiter Hector really liked us. I swear each pitcher of sangria was stronger than the last. "So all I'm saying is Nair does just as good of a job as waxing, you do it yourself and you don't have to tip," Naomi says, making her anti waxing point. "True, but Nair stinks. I told you about the girl in college that used Nair on her arm pits before we went to a party. She was worried you could smell it. When we got on the party bus, this girl yells out EWW it smells like Nair in here. She wouldn't throw her hands in the air all night," I say laughing while slapping my knee. Victoria decides to give some enlightenment. "Waxing isn't bad after the first time. You get used to it. The hair grows back thinner. Plus the girl that does mine is nice. I can talk to her about anything and she's so pretty." "Does she charge you extra for the flirting?" I ask jokingly. It was getting late so we decided to call it a night. Hector comes and gives us our bill. He didn't charge us for the 3rd pitcher of sangria. Since he was so nice we left a hefty tip.

As we walk to the door, we see this super drunk lady standing by the exit. The glass door in front of her was open, but for some reason she wanted to fight with the locked glass door next to it instead. I kept saying Miss, Miss, step this way. This door is open, but she was determined to go through that locked door. Finally after security stopped laughing they helped her out the opened door. We were hysterical. In the middle of us laughing our asses off I hear. "Hi! Excuse me hi. I don't mean to interrupt." I finally get control of myself and look up and there is this 6ft tall, bald, nice looking clean cut guy trying to get my attention. "I'm sorry," I say wiping tears from my eyes. "Did you see that lady? She fought with that door for 2 minutes," I say and start laughing again. "No I must have just missed it. I saw you inside with your friends. I didn't want to interrupt your meal, but I think you are beautiful," the nice gentleman says. Of course I am still laughing hysterically and barely hear anything he said. "I'm sorry what?" I say rudely. He repeats himself. "AWW thank you," I say as sweetly as possible. "My name is StickyFingers and you are?" he asked. "Hi I'm Shaunie." I honestly don't think I could be drier with my response. I was not looking to meet anyone that night. I was having a good time with my girls and to be honest I really needed a break from men. My track record these past two years was not good. Last thing I needed was another headache. "How old are you? Where are you from? What do you do for a living?" My line of questions shot out like bullets, but he was unbothered and answered like a champ. "I just turned 30 this year. I'm from Brooklyn and I'm a professor," he says proudly. "Oh brother you're younger and you're from Brooklyn? I can't." Seriously I could not be a bigger asshole until I said

85

"What's your background?" I kept seeing heads shaking and arms waving in my peripheral vision. It was Naomi and Victoria saying no, please don't be more rude. They were making subtle movements trying to point out how cute he was and that he had a nice height. Their sign language was sharp that night. "I'm half Cuban half Puerto Rican. Are you okay with that? What about you? How old are you? What's your background?" he asks laughing. "I'm 32 and black, are you okay with that?" I ask giving the side eye. "Really I thought you would have said Dominican. That's fine by me. I don't care about that stuff. You have beautiful eyes. Can we exchange numbers?" he asks awaiting my answer. Now I'm viewing him a little different. He's actually very handsome and built really nice. He speaks proper English, clean cut, he was a gentleman, and might I add extremely brave to interrupt a group of giggling tipsy women. "I have just one more question." I say. "Go ahead I have an answer." He replies. "Do you have any offspring?" he bursts out laughing. "You have a way with words. You are funny! No I don't have any children. Now take your phone out and put my number in it." I was impressed I did not intimidate him at all. This may be a good look. We exchange numbers and I warned him that I like to text, so I hope his typing game was strong.

Naomi and Victoria were hysterical. "If I was him, I would have walked away a long time ago. You were vicious," Naomi tells me. "You have to make them work for it sometimes, but real talk, you spit venom. He took it like a champ. You need someone that will challenge you. God I hope he has a license and a passport," Victoria sighs. "I'm not that bad. As long as he's not a mama's boy and really is single, we should do just fine," I say with a shoulder shrug.

The next day I'm feeling refreshed. I finally got a chance to sleep in on a Saturday morning. I didn't want to waste the day, but I didn't want to do too much because I had to work my overnight job later that evening. It's about 11am and I decide to make some breakfast and catch up on my DVR when all of sudden my phone alerts me I have a text. Oh here we go - it's StickyFingers.

StickyFingers: *Hello it's StickyFingers from last night. It was such a pleasure meeting such a beautiful woman.*

Me: *Good morning. It was nice meeting you as well.*

StickyFingers: *I was wondering if maybe we could go out sometime when I get back from vacation.*

Me: *I'm leaving for vacation as well. When do you get back? Sorry if I was rude last night BTW.*

StickyFingers: *September 1st. No worries you're a beautiful lady. I'm sure you get hit on all the time.*

Me: *Who told you that? I'm just kidding. You're right. :)*

StickyFingers: *I love your sense of humor.*

I ended up texting with StickyFingers all day and everyday up until I left for vacation. He was an open book and I liked that. I was used to guys who hid everything and he seemed very sincere. I had a great time on my cruise despite not finding a prince or a rich island guy. I was actually excited to get back. I was interested in getting to know StickyFingers better.

Our first date was this adorable Italian place in Brooklyn called Saraghina. We ordered two kinds of pizza and a big bottle of Pinot Grigio. "I have a really cool place to take you afterward," he says full of excitement as he continued. "It's a really cool bar and lounge. They have karaoke." I love when a man makes plans for me and guides me through the evening rather than constantly asking me what I want to do next. StickyFinger's was doing a great job leading. I was very impressed when he suggested karaoke.

I went through the massive book of karaoke songs looking for something for us to sing together, but he was too shy, so we decided to be enthusiastic audience members instead. As we walked back to my car I noticed he was walking on the correct side of the street, as any gentleman should. I unlocked the car door ahead of time as I could see he wanted to open it for me. I thought that was really sweet. The fact that he didn't have a car didn't bother me much. He was an absolute gentleman. I pulled up in front of his house to drop him off and along came the moment of truth. We agreed to see each other next week and said good night at least five times. He leaned in for a hug. As he pulled away slowly, he went for the kiss, and it was sweet, gentle and slightly wet. No one likes a person that tries to slobber your entire face, that's so gross. He did okay and had potential. Now I was intrigued.

StickyFingers and I were seeing each other for about a month and a half at this point. I think we might have eaten at every hipster restaurant Brooklyn had to offer. Fright Fest was going on at Great Adventures and I was dying to go. He thought it would be best if I spent the night at his place and we would leave from there in the morning. I got off my overnight job at 5 am and drove straight to his apartment. It would be my first time sleeping there. I was afraid I would be claustrophobic. StickyFingers lived in a studio apartment in his uncle's brownstone. The ceiling was low and he bumped his head on the light fixture more times then I'd like to remember. Although his living situation wasn't ideal for me, I respected the fact that he had his own place and kept it clean.

Now keep in mind it's 6am; at this point I have been up for 24 hours straight. All I wanted to do was sleep because I would be the only one driving to Great Adventures later that afternoon, but this man was feeling frisky. The spooning turned into heavy caressing, neck kisses and quite a few hand slaps from me. He eventually wore himself out. He controlled himself and even though I was slightly turned on I was annoyed just knowing I was the only driver. We got up around 1pm and decided to have brunch at Rustik Tavern before we headed out to Great Adventures. "Sorry about last night. You just smelled so good and you're just as gorgeous without makeup. I don't know what came over me," he said. "No worries, you said it's been awhile for you. Try my French toast it's amazing," I say with a wink. On our way to Great Adventures we played little road trip games and arrived there in no time.

We get to the ticket line and of course they offer their season pass deal. He bought 2. I was shocked. Most of the dudes

I've been to Great Adventures with were always looking for the soda can discount promotion. "We'll be back here," he says. I was excited and the best part was he wasn't afraid to ride the roller coasters. All I could think was: where have you been all my life?

On the drive back we were laughing about how he screamed like a baby on some of the rides and then my phone rang. I forgot to disconnect my Bluetooth. I look and it's Superman. I put my hands on 10 and 2 and cannot believe this is happening right now. I ignored the call and continued talking as if nothing happened. The phone rang again. Why, why is this happening? Without hesitation he says, "Um looks like Superman really wants to talk to you." I hit ignore again and say "Ha, ha that's funny so crazy ha!" I quickly turned up the music. "I love Usher. 'There goes my baaaaaby!'" I sing. He starts laughing at my desperate attempt to change the subject and sang along. Whew StickyFingers was a good egg. I drop off StickyFingers and decide to go home. I didn't want to spend the night with him because I wasn't in the mood to keep slapping his hands away all night. I really just needed some sleep and I wanted to wait. I feel sometimes sex complicates things. Plus I wanted to know why the hell Superman was calling me at 10 at night. Where was his baby mama? Where was the baby? I decided to text him at the red light.

Me: *Butt dialing gets people in trouble.*

Two minutes later my phone rings. It's Superman. "Ignoring phone calls gets people in trouble." "Well I went to Fright Fest so I couldn't talk," I say proudly. "Oh you had a date?

Excuse me. Look at you going on dates. Did he bring the soda can for a discount?" he says laughing. "No he bought us season passes. We're going back, so take that!" I brag. "No you won't," he says quickly, with confidence.

I laughed with Superman all the way home. We could talk about anything. One thing for sure we were definitely good friends.

It was the day of my event and I invited StickyFingers and a friend to attend. We had been dating for almost 3 months. He was really proving he could be boyfriend material, so I wanted to treat him to something really cool. It was a wine tasting so I warned him that he should eat heavily before he got there. He assured me he would pace himself and not to worry. When he arrived he looked so handsome. He wore slacks, a button shirt, a chunky cardigan with suede patches on the elbow and loafers. He really made an effort. I told him to meet me at registration so I could say hello and meet his friend. "Wow you look amazing," he tells me. "Thank you so do you. Did you eat? Remember to spit," I say. "Yes we're ready. My friend is a chef so he's a pro," he assures me. The night continues and he's constantly texting me.

StickyFingers: *Is there food here?*

Me: *Yes in the back.*

StickyFingers: *I don't feel like carrying this book can you get one for me later?*

Me: *No just take one at the end.*

StickyFingers: *Do you know the code for the Wi-Fi?*

Me: *No stop checking the Internet and taste.*

StickyFingers: *Where's the restroom?*

Okay I'm done and annoyed. I'm working. Why is he constantly texting me? He's drunk, he has to be drunk. Sabina and I walk inside to check on the vendors and we bump into StickyFingers. "Heeeeyy there you are beautiful. Want to try this?" he asks, offering his glass of wine. "No I can't. This is my friend Sabina. She's working with me tonight," I say annoyed. In true Sabina form she says "Hi hello, you guys look like you're having fun. Is this your first time?" StickyFingers says, "Yes!" He was very enthusiastic. "I can tell. Your teeth are stained. Clearly you haven't been spitting and rinsing," Sabina says sarcastically. I lean into StickyFingers and ask, "Are you drunk?" "No babe I'm fine seriously I'm good!" he assures me. I leave him and continue my vendor check. Everyone was happy so the countdown to get to my room and pass out was on. I wanted to kick off these heels and rip off this tight dress like the Hulk.

After a nice hot shower and a cup of tea, I organize my folders for tomorrow's events. As soon as my head hits the pillow, StickyFingers calls. "Hey you, listen I have a long day tomorrow. Are you home?" I ask. "Hey beautiful, I just wanted to let you know I was home. Thank you for the invite. Chef and I had a great time. He wants us to come to his restaurant for the red carpet treatment." "That sounds great. I really need to get some sleep. I'm sorry. I have to go." "Oh no it's okay, I understand, just one more thing before we get off the phone," he pleaded. "Okay hit me." "Um, is it okay that I took 3 wine glasses?" "You did WHAT? Why on earth would you do something like that? This is my job are you crazy?" I say, with steam coming out of my head. "I needed a set," he says. "You needed a set and you took 3?" I am beyond irritated. "I'm sorry I was drunk!" "Oh NOW you were drunk. When I asked you before if you were drunk you said no. So now you're a thief and a liar! I can't deal with this right now. I'm tired and I need to go to sleep. I have an early day. Have a good night," I say while pressing the hell out of the end button. Oh man, how I longed for the days when you could slam the phone down. It really solidified the anger.

There was only one person I knew that would be up at this time always ready to hear the shenanigans and that's Robyn. "Robyn you are not going to believe this shit," I say. "Uh oh who did it?" she asks. "StickyFingers just called me and told me he stole 3 wine glasses from my event," I say. "Are you fucking kidding me? Wait 3?" she asks confused. "Yeah he said he needed a set," I say. "And he took 3? WHAT?" she says. We both laughed hysterically for 2 minutes straight.

I decided not to take any of StickyFingers calls until my event was over. I was so angry and annoyed that he would be so foolish and so disrespectful. When the event weekend was over I called him on Monday and he was very apologetic, but I just couldn't get over it. "I can't believe you took those glasses. If you needed glasses why didn't you just ask me? That's like me coming into your classroom and stealing all the red Legos and telling you

93

yeah well my nephew needed a set. You would think I was crazy," I rant. "I'm really sorry it was stupid. I feel so stupid can we get past this?" he asks sincerely. "I'm sorry, I'm too rattled and just thinking of the possibilities of what could have happened if you got caught makes me so sick. Enjoy your set,." I say before I hung up the phone. I was so disappointed. We almost hit the 90 day mark. Sex wasn't a sure thing after 90 days, but I would have really started to consider it. He had so much potential to be a boyfriend. He was consistent, witty and a gentleman. Damn, online dating here I come.

#

Chapter 6: Online Dating Round 1: Applebee's King

"He was doing so well. I'm so mad at him. Who does that Naomi, really who?" I say whining over the phone. "Someone in desperate need of 3 wine glasses duh! Sorry that was too easy. Okay let's think about it. When you're under the influence, don't you start to think about all the stuff you need to steal?" Naomi asks laughing. "Are you done? It's not funny. Maybe I was too hard on him. I was thinking about giving him the cookie. I'm sad and horny now" I say laughing. "Oh stop it. Either let Superman dip in the cookie jar, or take your ass to the gym, or let StickyFingers steal your cookie" Naomi says cracking herself up. "I can't stand you. I'm going to the gym. Goodbye!"

I hung up with Naomi and chose the option of working out, but not by myself. I would just think too much. I called my girl Raquel. She loved taking spin and that's just what I needed. No talking, no thinking, just listening to the music and pedaling my little heart out. Raquel and I always shared our war stories about dating, work, and really just life in general. After class I was a sweaty mess. We decided to go get a smoothie so we could catch our breath while we cooled down. "So I had a second date last night with Wall Street guy. I think I'm starting to get past his lack of height," Raquel says really trying to believe herself. "Nice, wait is this the little guy from the dating site?" I ask. "Well yes and you're not helping me by calling him the little guy. I'm trying not to be shallow about it," she says. "Liking what you like is not shallow. I commend you for giving it a try. What dating site is he from?" I ask. "I found him on Match.com and can you believe I have a date every day this week? I wish you'd just sign up already. It's easy and will help you weed out the losers," she says convincingly. "Fine I will set up a profile tonight. I've put it off long enough. After what I've experienced just meeting someone by accident, I'm totally ready to meet someone on purpose. If the questionnaire part takes too long I'm not doing it" I say sternly. "Well that's the spirit, NOT. Ditch the 'tude girlfriend. You have to go in with a positive attitude and keep your mind open. Your Prince Charming is out there. There's nothing wrong with dating a few frogs on your journey to find him." Raquel makes me sick with her awesome analogies. She knows how much I love fairy tales. I was sold. She had me at Prince. "Yes my Prince Charming is out there. The poor idiot is probably stuck in a tree somewhere," I say rolling my eyes. "Go get 'em tiger!" she says as she slaps me on the back.

On the way home I convinced myself to at least download a dating app. I chose PlentyOfFish because it was free. I didn't feel comfortable spending money on a dating site just yet. I needed a practice run. I decided to take my time filling out the profile. I believe what's for me will be for me. I don't have to rush into this sea of lames hiding behind computer screens. Hmmm, that is certainly not the positive attitude Raquel was talking about. I decided to take a shower first so I would be comfortable when I got started.

Okay first question. If you could choose a super power what would it be? What is this kindergarten? I would totally teleport though. Going where I want when I want would be so cool. Okay maybe a glass of wine will help loosen me up and make this process less painful. What's the next question? What is your ideal vacation? Oh that's easy. I would say a private island far, far away with no cell phone service, so I can relax. Does that sound mean? Ugh delete. What's the next question? What would your mother say about you? Oh I got this one. Mom would say she needs to give me grand babies now ha-ha. Maybe that's too heavy delete. Oh okay upload picture here. That sounds simple enough. And that's all I did. I uploaded my picture and went to bed.

I woke up the next morning and my body was aching. I don't know what I was trying to prove on that bike yesterday. I check my phone and I have 167 notifications from this dating app. Who were these cyber men intrigued from one picture? I have to say, I gave myself a little high five for drawing that much attention. That picture did have good lighting. Wait until they get a dose of the great personality that goes along with that picture. Okay maybe I was feeling myself a little bit, but isn't that part of positive thinking? My mom always said if you don't think highly of yourself no one will. I'm ready to go fish.

I decided to check all these messages while commuting to work. The stars were definitely aligned because I got a seat on the crowded train and was able to scroll through these messages comfortably. The instructions seemed pretty simple. You swipe left if you don't like and right if you do like. Okay here we go. Who the hell would name themselves 2Hot2Handle69? Yuck, nice abs, but no. That's a left swipe for you mister. TheEducator, oh okay maybe he's a teacher. Oh no, no, no, I am not studying lap dancing sir. Why do you look so greasy in all of your pictures? Is that a tassel? Oh hell no left swipe. PurpleHazelEyes, hmm nice dreads. Oh would you look at that, your eyeballs really are hazel. Who are these kids? Caption reads: Me with some of my kids. SOME? There are four in the picture. Aggressive swipe left.

Okay, it is now clear to me that I'm going to have to fill out my profile completely. Maybe that will eliminate some of these clowns. My grandmother always said it's not the quantity it's the quality. So yes I got a ton of messages, but none worth responding to. Look at this, MisterSandman writes: "Hey gorgeous I love your profile, you're really smart, funny and just gorgeous. You want to take a nap together?" What? Is this dude serious? I didn't write anything. I am smart, but you can't get all that from a picture. Stop it and no I am not sleepy. EWW! Do the women on this site fall for this crap?

I filled out the questions little by little. The more information I added the better the prospects. Ha imagine that. When I finally finished writing about myself, it was time to submit what I was looking for. Okay female seeking male. No ethnicity preference, let's keep the options wide open. Yes she wants a 6 footer, but the height is negotiable pending on the personality. Usually guys that are less than 6ft tall have more personality. They have to make up for the lack of height somehow. Employed? You should most certainly be employed. How can you go on dates and not be employed? Children? Hmmm let's go with zero. I love the kids don't get me wrong, but if I have a choice to meet those without why not. Plus I would love to start our family together. You know let it be our first time, not you telling me everything that's going to happen in the delivery room ahead of time because that's what happened when junior was born. I'm just saying. It may sound petty, but like I said since I have a choice hey let's go for the gold. I will not let the zodiac dictate who I am compatible with. Please, please let him be a Leo, Sagittarius or Pisces. I like them a lot. Thirty to thirty-eight is a good age range. Not too young where he's still wet behind the ears, but not too old where his balls are sagging, he says things like give me five on the black-hand side, and he wears a ton of gold jewelry.

Okay I feel good about this. Let's see what we get. Gentleman4U hmm, okay cute picture. Let's read his message: "Hello gorgeous my name is AppleBee'sKing. I love your profile. Where are you from?" My reply was simple. "Hello AppleBee'sKing my name is Shaunie. I'm from New York. Were you born and raised in Virginia?" I hope he doesn't have a crazy southern accent. He's probably from Brooklyn and moved out there because the cost of living is cheaper. More bang for your buck. Or maybe he got in trouble with the law and he's hiding out with grandma until the coast is clear. Ugh I don't know about this? He lives so far away. Would he move back to NYC? I'm not moving out there. I have a career and big plans. I can't leave New York right now. Phew, down girl, breathe. Okay, okay relax he hasn't even replied yet. Oh here we go. "No I'm originally from Brooklyn. I moved out here after I graduated high skool." Shit I knew it, he's a king pin. I can't date a king pin. I've seen *Carlito's Way*, *Good Fellas*, *Casino*; it doesn't end well for the love interest. Did he spell school with a "K"?

"So you went to college out there or did you get in trouble with the law?" I think that was a gentle way to ask. He replies "You're pretty funny. No I came down here to stay with my uncle. He's older and needed help running his automotive shop. I ended up really liking it so I stayed. Kurrently I'm head of security for a few klubs out here." Oh okay well that explains that amazing body. Head of Security hmm, I wonder if that's a fancy way to say bouncer? "So how often do you visit NYC?" I ask. Let's face it if I'm going to even consider dating this man he will need to travel quite often. And what is up with his grammar? Where the hell is his auto correct? AppleBee'sKing: "I haven't been to NYC in a long time. It's been almost 3 years, but I am coming up for the holidays. Kould I take you out? Would that be kool?" OMG, OMG, OMG there goes those K's again. Okay pet-peeve alert: I don't mind shortening words or the occasional slang talk, but I'm worried this man really doesn't know when to use a "C" versus a "K". "Yes that would be cool. Currently I'm at work so I'll have to chat with you later. Hope you have a great day." I reply hoping he saw the correct spelling of my "C" words. He replied "Kay kool katch up wit u lata!" AWW damn!

I go on with my day totally concerned about this man's education. Perhaps he thinks it's cool to spell words wrong. Perhaps spelling is not one of his strengths. Granted I'm far from a spelling bee champ myself, but I'm pretty confident I know which words require a "C" versus a "K". I should keep looking just in case this guy is just pretty with a great body. Evry1LuvsRay, how cute is that name? Thirty seven, no kids, never been married, college grad, this is good. Seems normal so far. What's wrong with him? Why is he on here? Well, I'm on here, so we'll leave that question alone. Nice smile, good build, software engineer okay, okay. He's 5 feet 6 inches tall. Uh oh he's little, but that's okay. Maybe he's really funny. Birthday April 15th, whoop there it is. I can't date someone with the same birthday as me and you're vertically challenged too. No thank you. It would be too complicated. What happens when I'm ready to wear stilettos on my birthday and you want to play paint ball for yours? Me no likey. My birthday is the one day of the year I can celebrate me and focus on me without feeling guilty about it. If it's his birthday too then I'll be thinking about him and what to do for him. Oh hell no. I tried dating someone the same zodiac sign as me and even that was annoying. We both can't be bossy and nonchalant. There would be a lot of barking orders and nothing getting done in a timely manner. How does Raquel go on

101

so many dates? There are so many bad seeds. Maybe I am too picky. Look at this one from LetsPlayPapi: "Hey gorgeous. I know you're a little older, but I'm willing to be your boy toy. I've done it before and got no complaints." Yuck! And with that I just put the phone face down with pure disgust.

A few weeks have passed and I'm starting to get the hang of this online dating stuff. I haven't met anyone yet because I don't want to be cat-fished. I am talking to about six decent guys so I'll see how it goes with AppleBee'sKing before I schedule another date. Should I feel guilty talking to all these guys at once? A girl has to have back up right? I speak with AppleBee'sKing on the phone quite often and honestly I feel pretty comfortable talking to him. Texting is rather painful, but he has a nice voice and nice conversation. He tells me he wants to be married before he breeds. That's always a nice thing to hear from a guy. He's looking for something real and isn't into playing games. He thinks I could be the one. It all sounded great and had me very excited to meet him the next day. I can't believe he's driving all this way to stay for two days. This man was certainly about making his money so taking a day off from work was not an option for him. I respected his work ethic and liked that he was making time to see me during his short stay. I decided I should probably get some pointers from Raquel before my meet and greet, so I texted her.

Me: *Okay so I have been chatting with a few guys. One might be dyslexic, but he's nice, cute and has an amazing body and I'm meeting him tomorrow. Hey girl, how are you BTW?*

Raquel: *LOL Seriously? You know dyslexia is hereditary. Just think of* *your future child before you jump on that one.*

Me: Well it's better than tourettes. How is Hopkins by the way?

Raquel: You're such a jerk. I stopped speaking to Hopkins. I rubbed his leg during a foreign film and he yelled out "Squeeze my lemon balls."

Me: Wait what? LOL! So you dumped him. What's wrong? You don't like lemons? You're so mean. OMG that's hilarious!

Raquel: Ha, ha he said his tourettes only triggers when he's horny and well I'm hot so I didn't want to have that continuous pressure on him all the time. Poor guy. LOL.

Me: You're horrible. Well AppleBee'sKing is coming up to take me on a date. I don't know what to wear.

Raquel: Oh this is exciting. Be cute and comfortable. Don't wear anything too tight or you may discover he has tourettes and may want to squeeze your cantaloupes.

Me: LOL girl stop they're more like grapefruits I think.

Raquel: LOL you're so funny. Make sure you meet early evening in a populated place in case he's a nut job. Don't be scared I'm sure it will go great oh and pack your mace.

Me: I don't have mace. I have travel hairspray.

Raquel: Close enough. Good luck Chica! And be positive.

How do you tell me not to be scared and pack mace all in the same sentence? This girl was hilarious.

AppleBee'sKing sent me a message saying he was heading up and should arrive in NYC in 6 hours. I can't believe this is really happening. In less than 24 hours I would be on my first online date. I decided to go to bed early. I had a hot date and I had to go to my second job afterward. If the date went well I would call out. If not I would have my girls text me about an emergency and well I'll just get to the second job early.

Saturday morning I wake up around 11am. I decide to take it easy because I had a long evening ahead of me. AppleBee'sKing arrived in NYC safely and was visiting his family. He told me how excited he was to see me in person. We FaceTimed sporadically, but clearly it's not the same. He told me he wanted a big hug and all I kept thinking was please, please let him smell clean.

I decided to wear jeans a cute top and some high boots. Sexy casual was what I was going for. We were going to meet in New Roc City. There's a movie theatre, arcade, and plenty of places to eat. I arrive at New Roc and I'm so nervous. My girls were on standby ready to save me. At 4pm I received a text from him.

AppleBee'sKing: *Hey gorgeous I'm here. Where r u?*

Me: *I'm here hiding in my car. I don't see you.*

AppleBee'sKing: *LOL I'm hiding in the arcade. Let's count to 3 and come out.*

Me: *Okay deal.*

I stand by the entrance way waiting to see if he walks up and finally this little muscled man in a hooded sweatshirt walks out and stands near the benches. He's cute, but way smaller than I expected. "AppleBee'sKing?" I ask trying to pretend we walked out simultaneously. "Shaunie? Oh my goodness you are even prettier in person. Wow! Bring it in and give me a hug girl," he says with his arms wide open. Okay here it goes. I go in for the hug and I have to admit he's a great hugger and he smells amazing. He had these long beautiful eyelashes. Girls pay for lashes like those. He was definitely a good looking guy, but he was short. 5'10" my ass. "Pretty and you smell good too. Wow! I'm a lucky dude right now," he says as he squeezes me tighter. Now I'm uncomfortable. I think he may have tried to flex his muscles during the embrace. I don't know my ear felt weird during the hug. It was too tight.

"Okay, okay we can't sit here and hug the whole time mister. What should we do? There's the theater, there's the arcade, or do you want to just grab something to eat?" I say trying to get this show on the road. "Oh okay it's whatever you want to do beautiful. I'm down for whatever you know. It's all about you," he says as he strokes his beard very pimp-like. I was a little annoyed at his mannerisms. I guess he was trying to be funny or at least I hope he was. I was also bothered that he didn't have a plan. I can't stand an indecisive man. Call me old fashion, but I like a man to lead. I'm single. I make all the decisions for me all the time. It would be nice to let someone else take the reins. "Um how about we see a movie? Are you familiar with 'The Hunger Games'? The second part, 'Catching Fire' is out and I'd like to see it," I suggest. "Yeah that's cool I heard of it. I mean I don't know the storyline all that well, but yeah let's do it. As long as I'm with you it's cool," he says with a smile and he does that pimp like beard stroke again. Maybe he's nervous. I'm not sure, but my patience was wearing thin. For me there weren't any sparks yet and that frustrated me, especially since we'd had such great phone conversations.

He paid for the movie and bought me a kid's snack pack. Don't judge me. You get popcorn, a drink and candy for under $5. It's genius. We get in the theater and of course he suggests I pick the seat. It was pretty crowded so I chose two seats on the end near the exit. You know just in case I had to make the great escape. Twenty minutes into the movie he was asleep. Twenty-two minutes into the movie he was asleep with his mouth wide open and snoring. I got up and moved over one seat. He was pretty loud. The movie was great and he did not wake up once. While the credits rolled I moved back to my original seat next to him and gently nudged his shoulder. He wakes up and says, "That was a great movie. Did they catch all the fire? I missed the end sorry it was a long drive?" It was at that moment that I figured out that this man was all looks. He should practice being the good looking silent type. "Um yeah it was a great movie. Um I have to go to the restroom. I'll meet you in the front," I say rushing out of the theater. I get to the bathroom and check my phone. Everyone texted me to make sure I was okay.

Mom: *How's it going? Do you want me to come get you?*

Raquel: *Is he cuter in person? Does he have **tourettes?***

Robyn: *Hey Chica. Just let me know you're alive before I come to New Roc with swat.*

Naomi: *Robyn is about to call swat. I'm prepared to call my people...they're not afraid to go to jail. Text me back.*

Brother: *Why is Ma asking for my Louisville Slugger? Call that woman please.*

I love my friends and family. I texted everyone back to let them know I was okay and would be going to work later. Unfortunately AppleBee'sKing did not entice me to call out. I head to the front to meet him and he's standing there looking really confused. "I didn't see Lenny Kravitz in the movie. Did you?" he says puzzled. "Um listen I have to go to work in a few hours. Did you want to get something to eat or should we call this a night? It's 6:15 pm now so I'm fine either way really," I say trying not to sound annoyed. "No let's eat gorgeous. I don't want you to go to work hungry. What's around here? Let's see, let's see, OOOOOHHHH APPLEBEE'S!!! You want Applebee's? I love APPLEBEE'S! They have such great deals. Back in VA I go at least twice a week. I mean not unless you want something else. You okay?" he asks. I cannot imagine the shocked look that must have been on my face as he expressed his love for this restaurant. I could not believe how excited he was to eat at Applebee's. It's like he transformed into a big kid. He had pep in his step. Eyes were wide open. He certainly wasn't sleepy anymore. What the hell was going on?

"Um sure yeah we can go. You seem so happy about it," I say sarcastically. The sarcasm flew over his head. He gave me a big smile, put his arm around me and guided me to Applebee's. He whispers to me, "I'm going to get us a booth. I know how you girls love booths." EWW. Pet-peeve alert number two: Don't tell me what I like and generalize me with some made up statistic. Granted I love sitting in booths, but to just assume and not ask ugh, what a chauvinist. There would be a 20 minute wait for the booth and well I didn't have that kind of time so we opted for two seats in the back.

The waiter gives us our menus and asks for our drink order. "You're not getting alcohol right? I mean since you have to work?" The way he asked led me to believe that 1) He didn't want me to drink because he doesn't drink or 2) Funds were limited. I was not convinced he was concerned about me working under the influence. "I'll have water and a glass of strawberry lemonade," I say to the waiter. The waiter smiled and gave me this wide eye what the hell is wrong with this guy stare. So to lighten the awkwardness, I asked AppleBee'sKing to tell me something I didn't know about him. He says, "Well that's hard. I don't really like talking about myself. How do I look in person? Usually I get compliments on my long lashes and biceps. I did double work in the gym before coming to see you. What do you think?" He waits patiently for my response. As I stare at him, I think to myself, "Wow, he functions in society." Our conversations on the phone were always very simple. He never talked about future plans other than marrying me, and honestly, right now those pretty looks of his weren't so intriguing.

"Here are your lemonades. Are you guys ready to order?" the waiter asks. "Hey, are those lemonades with free refills? AppleBee'sKing asks. "Yes they are." The waiter replies giving me that wide eyed look again. "Oh cool, okay yeah um you know what you want? We can split something. The two for $20 deals are pretty great here. Even the two for $25 deals are still good. You like pasta?" AppleBee'sKing says to me. The waiter snickers and I say gesundheit to cover up the fact that he's clearly laughing at AppleBee'sKing. I'm sure he's wondering how I'm even still sitting here. "You pick. I'm allergic to seafood so go for it," I say. "Okay cool we'll take two pastas with chicken on this two for $20 side of the menu. Thank you." He hands the waiter both our menus, leans in and says, "That's my favorite. Best thing on the menu."

"So I have to say when I first saw you my immediate thoughts were he's smaller in person. Like in your pictures you look like the Hulk, but in person you're not scary big at all." I sip my lemonade waiting for his reply. His entire body sulked as if I insulted him. I wasn't trying to be rude. I was just being honest. "What's wrong? You have a great body. Are you trying to be scary big?" I sip more of my lemonade. "No I'm just used to women telling me how big I am. When I used to strip they would always tell me that during a lap dance." And that's when our waiter came rushing over to me slapping me on my back because I was choking and the tears were running out of my eyes uncontrollably. After I assure the entire restaurant I am fine and did not need medical assistance. I ask, "So what was or is your stripper name?" This time I waited before I put food in my mouth for his answer. He leaned in and said "Big Tasty." I simply smiled and waved the waiter over to give us the check. Shockingly he reached for the check and paid for the meal. We get to the parking lot and he walks me to my car. "I had a really nice time. I hope I can see you again," he says reaching for a hug.

I hug him. After all he did smell great, but I had to be honest. "We'll see. I mean don't get me wrong my body is really, really, really attracted to your body, but when you speak my brain gets very angry." I left him standing there pondering what that meant and got into my car. First online date was a wash, but I won't let it discourage me. I was moving on to the next candidate. Anything has to be better than this.

"Wait, soooo he never mentioned being a stripper before? Are you sure?" Robyn asked laughing hysterically over the phone. "That's not something you miss Robyn. I'm not judging him. I just think he could have mentioned that earlier. Can we talk about how I almost died in the restaurant?" I say. "Oh my goodness. I can't stop laughing Shaunie. Wait, wait soooo what would have happened if the lemonades didn't come with free refills?" Robyn asks trying her hardest not to laugh. "I'm glad you're so amused. I don't know he probably would say I should only have one, you know since I had to go to work and all," I say sarcastically. "I can't breathe. Literally there are tears coming from my eyeballs. I'm hysterical. This guy was so funny. So wait whose next?" Robyn asks. "I'm not sure," I say.

While I scroll through the various prospects on the PlentyOfFish app, my phone sends me a notification that I have a Facebook message. "I have a Facebook message Robyn. How is that possible? I never use this thing. My boss had me create a profile to promote work events, but we have an online team for that now," I say totally annoyed. "Can you read the message without logging in? You know I stay away from Facebook. I don't know how it works," Robyn says. "Shut the front door.

You will not believe who the message is from. I forgot all about this guy. Some people just can't stay gone. I mean really it's been over 10 years," I say in shock. "Tell me, tell me, tell me!" Robyn says with excitement. "Okay are you sitting? It's DramaKing!" I say, anticipating her reaction. Robyn responds with, "EWW why?"

#

Chapter 7: Blocking the DramaKing

"I hardly remember DramaKing. You two dated briefly the summer of our sophomore year right? You went back to school and that was it. Oh and DramaKing was hella cheap," Robyn recalls. "Yeah sounds about right. I think that may have been one of the reasons we stopped speaking. I mean let's be real here. How many times can a lady go for a stroll in the park? Do I look like my name is Clifford?" I say cracking myself up. "Wait the dog? Ha! I can't with you," Robyn says laughing. "Oh how I don't miss the days of being a broke college student. We were all in the struggle back then. Maybe things changed. He could have a helicopter now and be the CEO of a major company," I say dreaming big as usual. "Are you willing to find out?" Robyn asked. "YES!! You know I believe in signs. God will put people in your life as a blessing or a lesson. Let's see what he is," I say sounding hopeful. "Okay, but keep in mind you may be the blessing for him and he may be the lesson for you. Be careful little miss hopeless romantic," Robyn warns. "You are wise grasshopper. I'll tread lightly. He has a good profile picture though," I say, nodding with approval. "And so it begins. Good luck Chica!" Robyn says.

As I hung up with Robyn I couldn't help but think: what if she's right? What if he's just a lesson? Why did we stop speaking? I feel like he was charming, but an asshole. I would have never thought to reach out to him, now that I'm really thinking about it. I don't even know how to respond to this message.

DramaKing: Pretty Brown eyes how are you??

Hmm, what's wrong with you again? That's what I really wanted to ask. I really hate wasting my time. Let me think. How many times have I tried to date someone from my past and it was successful? ZERO SHAUNIE ZERO! I'm so hard headed. So I responded.

Me: Hey you it's been a long time.

I am a hopeless romantic so I gave him my contact info. Wouldn't that be a cool story to tell the kids? "Your father and I lost contact and he looked for me on social media. We saw each other and have been together ever since." As I continue to day dream, my phone sends me an alert. I have a new email, and wouldn't you know it, it was DramaKing.

DramaKing: I can't believe I found you. I tried looking for you before, but no luck. How have you been? Still beautiful I see.
Me: Thank you, still charming I see. Yeah it's been a long time. I'm doing well. I have an event coming up. Would you like to attend?
DramaKing: I won't be able to make that, but I would still like

113

to see you.

I gave DramaKing my number. I was curious to know what he had been up to after all these years. He called me that evening and we were on the phone for hours. He works in finance, which totally makes sense with his history of being a cheap skate. Never been married, no kids, and lived alone. He loved to travel and liked eating out. He was 6'4", slim build, and dark chocolate. He swore he favored Tyson Beckford. I didn't see it, but he was certainly handsome with pretty white teeth. We decided that we were going to meet up quickly before I went to my second job. He was trying to figure out the bus route to get to me. He said there were no cabs around, so me, being the kind-hearted person I am, picked him up. As he's waiting to cross the street, a little old lady walked up next to him. Of course he helped her cross the street. He sees me watching him help the lady and he winks at me. I gave a smirk. He was still a ham. He gets in the car and gives me a hug. He smelled amazing and was dressed so adorable with a button up and slacks. We went back to my apartment, had some wine, and talked some more. Before I knew it, the make out session was on. He was always a good kisser. It was getting pretty steamy and I had to shut it down for 3 reasons: 1) there was no way he would be getting my cookie so easily. He would have to earn that. 2) I had to go to work. And 3) please refer back to reason 1. "Can you call out? I want us to spend more time together," he says so sincerely. "As much as I would love to I can't. It's time to make the donuts," I say as I jump up to go change my clothes. "Well I'll ride downtown with you. I don't want to leave you." It was at that moment I remembered how inseparable we were that summer way back when. We saw each other at least 4 times a week. My mother even let him spend the night because he stayed over so late. Of course, she would threaten his life if he moved off that couch in the middle of the night, but she still let him stay. "Wow! Are you sure? That's a long ride on the train coming back," I said, quite shocked. "That doesn't bother me. I want to catch up some more," he said, holding my hand.

He rode with me to lower Manhattan and I have to say having the company was actually nice. Usually while riding alone I would sing loudly to whatever was playing on the radio. It was nice to hold a pleasant conversation before pulling an all-nighter.

After that day, we saw each other almost every weekend. He would get his hair cut and hangout with me afterward. If we weren't together we would FaceTime. He was extremely comfortable in my home. He was there quite often. I started considering giving him the cookie, but there was something that really bothered me about him. He was such a secret squirrel. He never invited me to his place and he refused to tell me where he worked. Apparently some young girl he was seeing cheated on him and broke his heart. His trust issues were ridiculous. He wanted to know everything about me but shared minimal information about himself. It's funny how when you're all excited and wrapped up into someone, your vision is so blurry. It's not until you step back and really start paying attention, that you start to notice the cracks in the foundation.

T.D. Jakes says, "You'd be surprised at the things that look great on the outside, but are dysfunctional on the inside. Be sure to function as good as you look."4 Behind closed doors, dysfunction was running rampant in this man. Always trust your gut, right? DramaKing became more distant as I became more inquisitive. My goal was to level the playing field and find out what was going on with him. He wouldn't answer his phone for weeks. When he finally called me, I was shopping. He had the nerve to get an attitude with me for not calling him on his birthday. After all, all of his Facebook friends said happy birthday. Whether he was joking or not, I was not in the mood for his dry-ass sense of humor. Isn't it ironic how when you like someone their jokes are so funny and when you don't like them anymore all their jokes are corny? I asked what the hell his problem was and why did he ignore me for so long. He told me he was sick and when he's not feeling well he's moody and doesn't want to be bothered. After I cursed him out ever so lady-like in the bedding section of Home Goods for being so rude and inconsiderate, I decided to block his ass. I didn't do anything to him to ever deserve that kind of treatment. I don't care how you treat everyone else. You don't group me with others. I would love to say he remained blocked, but that was the first of many times. It was like I blocked him every few months. I thought maybe my absence would make him grow up, get himself together, be more open, but unfortunately each time was worse than the last.

"So what's going on with the dating sites? How's your weekend house pest, I mean guest? I miss you. Tell me everything," Naomi says over the phone. "I took a break from the dating sites and that house pest has been blocked again. Every time I speak to him he's asking me if I cooked. If I say yes, the follow up question is do I want company? If I say no the follow up is I'm so tired I got off so late today. Something is wrong with him. If I suggest hanging out he's got a ton of things to do. When I ask if he ended up doing any of the things he was planning on doing, he says no, he was lazy and slept. He's either seeing someone, a user, or just a complete asshole," I say with a long weary sigh. "I'll take all of the above for $300 Alex. I'm sorry baby cakes, but that's not good at all. Men are supposed to lighten your load not increase it," Naomi says smacking on something. "Load? I hate laundry. Bad analogy and what are you eating?" I ask. "Le Boyfriend bought me Chipotle. Don't be judging me. This burrito is everything to me right now. I want to kick Aunt Flow in the throat." "I hate that heifer. She pops up every 28 days like clock-work. 26 days if she's feeling herself and wants to ruin my plans," I say laughing. "Exactly she's the worst. And for the record I don't like DramaKing. He's a piece of shit. I hate that you always unblock him," she says sounding extremely annoyed. "You don't like anybody. You just want me all to yourself," I say giggling. "I don't care, I don't care, I don't care.

So what if I do? But seriously, I'm going to keep it real with you because you would do the same for me," Naomi begins.

"DramaKing doesn't deserve your kindness. You've cooked for him, let him stay in your house when he was sick, you've taken him out for his birthday, you've treated him to dinner and for what? What has he done for you? He's hung out with your family on numerous occasions. Have you hung out with his? NO you haven't." "He treated me to a movie," I say interrupting. "Oh right and when you asked if he was going to feed you afterward he said what?" Naomi asked. "He said he only said movie," I say with a sigh. "Exactly, I know you're Miss Independent and all, but that's fucked up. You like the fact that he's around when you have a break in your busy-ass schedule. He has nothing but time because he doesn't do shit. There's not one ambitious bone in his body. And let's not forget the numerous times he has called you in the middle of the night, telling you he took the wrong train and he's in your neighborhood. Then has the audacity to ask if he could sleep on your couch. Which I think is complete bullshit by the way. Who continuously takes the wrong train? He's either doing that shit on purpose to see if someone is in your apartment or he needs to stop drinking because clearly he can't seem to find his way home. How about how he's forever telling you he wants you to be the mother of his kids, and then tells you about all the chicks that flirt with him. Or how he innocently gave his number out to a co-worker that's trying to sleep with him? I for one am glad you stopped speaking to him. He's like a chick. He's always trying to be in your business. He's too nosey and he took advantage of your nurturing nature. Please stop talking to him. You can't fix everyone Shaunie. Who are you, Captain Save-a-Lame Ass?" Naomi concludes her speech. "I wish I had a rebuttal, but you're right. I am a fixer. I honestly think he's depressed, but that's assuming, because he doesn't let me in. I can't confirm it. I'm just curious as to how someone could be so up one day and down the next. It's so weird," I say confused. "Well curiosity killed the cat baby cakes. Give it up. Just for shits and giggles what happened this time?" Naomi asked.

Sunday I was supposed to take my Grandma to the movies. She wanted to see a Kevin Costner movie that came out in the theater a while ago. I was finally able to find a theater still playing it. She's an early bird so a matinee would be best. I give her a call around 9 am to see if she'll be ready in an hour. "Good morning Sunshine. I found the movie. It's in a theater in Port Chester. Can you be ready in an hour?" I ask. "Well what's shaken bacon? Hell no, I can't be ready in an hour. How far is that and do we have to take the highway?" Granny asked. "Well you picked a movie that's only in selected theaters. You can pick something else, but know you will be on a highway," I say. "Yeah I don't know. I'm feeling lazy. We should reschedule. Nothing is really out and I hate highways anyway. All those trucks and people merging like they've lost their minds, makes me uncomfortable. Hey why don't you invite DramaKing?" Granny says teasing. "I haven't really been speaking to him. I guess it could be an icebreaker, since we're supposed to be friends. I take him in small doses," I explain. "I told you he's like a woman. He's too nosey. He's too involved in your business. I told you about going backwards. You left it behind for a reason. Why do you want to be friends? You need to start telling him to mind his own business. He should be treating you to the movies as often as he tries to monopolize all your time with his bullshit. Child let me get off this phone, he just worked my last nerve. Call me later," Granny says as she hung up the phone. He totally can have that effect on people.

I grabbed my iPad and decided to FaceTime him. "Good morning! Would you like to treat me to a movie today?" I ask as playfully as possible. "Good morning!" he laughs, then continued. "What movie are you trying to see Fifty Shades?" he says sarcastically. "No actually I would like to see 'Into the Woods' with Meryl Streep, interested?" I ask. "Yeah I guess we could do that. I just have to do a few chores and go to Manhattan to drop something off. I should be done around 3pm." "That's too late. Maybe we can try another time," I say. "What time were you trying to go?" he asked. "Right now, during matinee time. It would be quick, early, and fun," I say, getting motivated to go out again. "Okay let me get up. I definitely have to get these chores done before I go," he says. "How about we do this? I have some errands to run. When I'm done, I will check on you to see how you're doing with time. If you're done we will head out; if not I will go on with my day. Cool?" I say sounding enthusiastic. "Okay we'll see," he says. And with that, I end the FaceTime call. I decided to make myself a nice breakfast, before heading to the grocery store.

As soon as I start getting dressed about an hour later, I got a confusing text from DramaKing. What I understood from it was that he was flaking again and giving me another lame excuse explaining why. I didn't get mad. I didn't care because it was his m.o.; I was so used to it and beyond over it. Somehow, during the back and forth, the conversation took a sharp left turn, as he basically accused me of using him to pay for this matinee movie. Apparently, he was bothered by the way I had asked him to the movie. His text came off as if he was scolding me on proper etiquette. I quickly realized why I had blocked him so many times before.

This rant went on and on. I stopped responding and still it continued. I finished getting dressed and I went to visit my mother. She's been telling me to pick up this lasagna she made for the past 2 days now. I get to my mother's house and she immediately heated up the lasagna. She was going to make sure I ate that lasagna, come hell or high water. While we're eating and catching up on reality TV, my phone beeps again. "What is with you and your brothers with these noisy phones? Who is that? I'm being nosey and I don't care. I'm your mother," she says with her nose in the air. "You say that every time you ask about something that's none of your business," I say giggling. "Just because I don't pay the bill doesn't mean I can't know. So who is it?" she asks again. "It's DramaKing, being an ass," I say as I roll my eyes. "Oh tell him to kick rocks. He's annoying. He's always nagging. Why do you like him huh? Why? Is it because he's tall? Girl, get

121

over it! More height just means, more dumb, dumb," she says, and we both start laughing. "Now go tell him to jump off a curb. You're busy," she says, cracking herself up. We continue to watch TV and I put my phone on silent.

Around 2pm I headed to the grocery store. I was finishing up at the check-out line when my phone vibrated. It was DramaKing. "Hello," I say unbothered. "Hey what's up? Did you go to the movies?" he asks. "What do you care anyway? You weren't trying to go remember," I say sarcastically. "No, it's not that I wasn't trying to go, it's the way you asked me that was the problem," he explains. "If you had a problem with it, then you should have said no. Not give long dragged-out explanations and bullshit examples like I'm some child," I said. "I was just trying to get my point across," he says, as I interrupt with "I don't care about your point. It was pointless. You're mean. So stop calling me and leave me alone. You're always trying to justify your fucked up behavior. You said 'treating' should be done 'naturally.' Well, since I'm not the woman that makes you want to 'treat naturally' then leave me alone. Let's not waste each other's time," I say calmly. "I'm not saying..." was all I heard. I hung up on him. He started texting more bullshit, but I just ignored it.

"He's horrible. Why do you deal with him?" Naomi asked. "I don't know. He was so easy to talk to in the beginning, but I can't explain it," I say confused. "Let me tell you what your gift and curse is. You're able to find that little bit of good in someone and hold on to it. Regardless of what they do to you, you still hold on to the bit of good you witnessed way back when. What you need to realize is, when someone shows you who they really are, believe them. The bad had to have out-weighed the good by now. I tell you what: Saturday after next let's go out," Naomi says. "Actually my friend Emerson invited me to go dancing with a few of his friends. You remember Emerson right?" I ask. "Yes, yes he's so adorable. I love the way he dresses. Does he have a boyfriend yet? He's so cute," she squeals. "No, but he's on the hunt… hence the dancing. Come with us. At least we don't have to worry about getting hit on," I say. "I'm in, let's do it!" Naomi says all excited.

A couple of weeks go by and DramaKing and I are cordial. Yes I unblocked him. I promised him I would help him prep for an upcoming job interview. "Are you sure they are going to ask me that?" DramaKing asks. "How the hell should I know? I found these questions on the internet,." I say. "Okay, okay, ask me another one." "No I'm done. I have to get dressed," I say. "Oh okay, where are you going?" "None of your business," I say, proud of myself for letting the words flow so easily. "What's the big deal? I don't care if you're hanging out with a guy. We're friends right?" "It's not a big deal. It's just none of your business. And for the record, you and I have very different definitions on friendship. I have to go," I say sternly. "Ah come on, how long are you going to be downtown?" "None of your business!" I reply once again. "Ah, so you are going downtown. Where? I'm going out tonight too." "I don't care where you're going. Goodbye," I say as I end the FaceTime call.

I get dressed and I head over to Naomi's to pick her up. "You look yummy. Hey pooh bear!" Naomi says as she gets into the car. "So do you hot stuff! So happy you're coming out. It's been too long. Let's hit it. Seat belts!" I say as we take off into the night. "What is this place called?" Naomi asks in the middle of her singing. "Pulqueria!" I say bopping my head to the music. "You can't be serious right now! Poltergeist what?" she says laughing. "We are heading to Pulqueria, silly. At first I thought it was a gay lounge, but it's just a Mexican restaurant lounge in Chinatown," I say laughing. Luck would have it that "It's Raining Men" would start playing on the radio. Naomi and I looked at each other with straight faces before we belted out "Hallelujah" and sang along.

We had such great time at the club. We danced all night. "I hope the DJ calls Emerson. They look like they would be cute together," Naomi says as we walk back to the car. "Yeah I can't believe he was bold enough to…uh oh Superman just texted me," I say as I read my text message. "He's texting you at 2 o'clock in the morning? Did you two have plans young lady?" Naomi asks, giving me her suspicious eye squint. "No. I mean, well I told him we could hang some time, but not today. What the hell?" I say, slightly confused.

Superman: *Where are you? I need to see you.*

Me: *Pardon? I'm out in these streets. Thuggin'.*

Superman: *When will you be home?*

Me: *Around 3ish I guess why? Are you okay?*

Superman: *I'll meet you there.*

Me: *Um excuse me sir I didn't invite you.*

Superman: *Are you expecting company?*

Me: *No, but you can't just invite yourself to my apartment.*

Superman: *Since when? See you around 3.*

"Oh my, oh boy, oh my!" I say panicked. "What, what happened? What did he say?" Naomi asks. "He said he's coming to my house and he needs to see me now. I don't know what's going on. My texts were pretty funny. Can you believe he didn't type LOL once?" I say with a pout. My phone was dying and the USB wire for my car was not working so I couldn't charge it. Then my phone started to ring. "Oh no it's DramaKing," I say. "Let's see what this jerk wants," Naomi says as she answers the call. My Bluetooth connected the call to my car speaker. "Hello Mr. DramaKing. How can I help you this morning?" I ask sarcastically. "Hey I'm still downtown. Where are you?" he asks. "Uptown!" Naomi yells. "Who was that?" DramaKing asks laughing. "None of your business. Why are you calling me sir?" I ask. "No, I figured we could meet up and ride uptown together," he says. "No I'm not picking you up to take you home. Nice try!" I say. "OMG hang up, is he serious?" Naomi whispers. I just looked at her, shook my head, pretended my fingers were a gun and put them to my temple. She pretended her fingers were guns too and said "Bang, Bang." We started laughing. "I can't believe you shot me," I said to Naomi. "Shot you? Huh? What?" DramaKing asked. "It's the only way to end this call," Naomi yells as she pushes the "End Call" button and disconnects DramaKing. We could not stop laughing. My phone died so I couldn't call back even if I wanted to. "So what does Superman want? Ooh is it a booty call? You're giving up the cookie!" Naomi sings. "Oh no, we are just friends and he's engaged now. In fact he set a date so it's going down. I'm staying away," I say, throwing my hands in the air as if to surrender. "Please keep both hands on the wheel. One more time won't hurt. Not unless you like it rough. Ayo," Naomi says as we pull up to her apartment. "Listen, charge your phone and text me when you get home. As a matter of fact, call me. And remember, I know low people in high places. I will have Superman and DramaKing's ass on the back of a milk carton," she says, trying to hold a serious face. "What? They don't put missing adults on… girl get out!" I say laughing. "Bye baby cakes and thanks for a good time. Don't forget to text me," Naomi says. "Toodles noodles!" I say, as she gets out the car.

I find parking right in front of my building and there is Superman's black Jeep Cherokee parked right across the street. I walk up to the truck slowly and peek in the window. His seat was reclined back and he was lying there with his eyes closed. He had definitely been drinking. I gently knock on the window and he pops up, sees me, and immediately gets out the car. "Hi," he says as he takes my hand and leads me up the stairs to my building. We go inside and I immediately go to my room to plug in my phone. I come back into the living room to find Superman pacing back and forth. I ask "What's going on?" "Would you lie to me?" he asks. "Excuse me?" "Would you lie to me?" he asks again. "No I wouldn't. Just tell me already!" I say nervously.

"I want to leave my girl and be with you. I've been thinking about this for a long time now and I just can't get you out of my system. We click, you get me, and I want to know that if I say I'm telling her tonight I'm leaving, you will say 'I got you' and we can make us work?" As I stare at him, I'm at a loss for words. Just as the tears began to fill my eyes, my intercom rings. Who the hell is ruining my moment? I thought to myself. "Who the hell is that?" Superman asks. "I don't know, probably someone hit the wrong bell," as I try to get back to my moment. "I don't know what to say. Are you serious right now?" I ask as the intercom rings again. "Who is that Shaunie? Are you expecting company? I asked you if you were expecting company earlier. Are you?" he asks irritated. "No I'm not expecting company. I told you it's the wrong bell." Just as I say that my phone starts ringing. Are you kidding me right now? "So let me guess. You want me to believe that call is a wrong number?" Superman asks sarcastically.

I get up and check my phone and it's DramaKing calling me. What the hell did he want? I ignore the call and go back into the living room to find Superman drinking a glass of water. How the hell did he go in my refrigerator so fast and where was my glass? "Who was that?" he asks. "Nobody, listen I don't think ..." I'm interrupted by the intercom ringing again, followed by DramaKing's text tone blaring from my phone. I check and there are a bunch of text messages.

DramaKing: *Are you home? I took the wrong train.*

DramaKing: *I'm coming to your house.*

DramaKing: *Answer the door. I see your lights are on.*

DramaKing: *I see your car outside. Why won't you answer the door?*

The intercom rings again and Superman comes into the bedroom. "Do you want me to answer that? You want me to go downstairs. I'm getting tired of this shit. I asked you if you were expecting company Shaunie. What the fuck?" he says pissed. "Um can you stop pacing back and forth please? You're making me nervous. Please go sit down and calm down. Everybody just calm down!" I yell as I leave the room panicking. Superman is hot on my heels. "Shaunie, who is that ringing the intercom? Is it DramaKing? Huh is it?" he asks. "Yes it's DramaKing, but I didn't invite him here. I don't know what he's doing here," I say nervous as hell. "I just asked you if you would lie to me Shaunie and now dudes are just popping up at your house. Why does he feel comfortable enough to come to your house unannounced?"

I paused for a minute because I was taken aback by the question. I was the King of this castle since I paid all the bills by myself. How ironic: I could have asked him the same question. It was clear to me he was under the impression he ran shit in here. As I was about to answer, I hear a soft tap at my window. There it goes again and again. What the hell is that? I could not figure out that noise. "Are you fucking serious? This dude is throwing rocks at your window," Superman says laughing. "OMG this is not happening. I can't believe this. He took the wrong train. He's drunk. I need a nap. I'm very overwhelmed right now!" I shout. "You're overwhelmed? I come here to tell you I love you and want to be with you, and you got dudes ringing your bell at 4 o'clock in the morning. How do you think I feel? I feel stupid, that's how I feel Shaunie."

I start crying because I feel terrible. This man that I've secretly loved for so long finally confessed that he loved me too. "I love you. I've loved you for a long time. I didn't say anything because I didn't want you to think I was crazy. I try to date other guys and I compare them all to you," I say crying. He holds me while I sob into his chest. Finally it's quiet. No more intercoms buzzing. No more phones ringing. It's just me crying into this man's amazing chest. "Look at me," he says. "Maybe I should have told you sooner and we wouldn't be in this mess. Now what do we do?" "You should go home and be with your fiancé and live happily ever after. Maybe one day we will be friends. I told you before that we will be together in the next lifetime. As much as I would love to run off into the sunset with you, I can't. The grass is not always greener on the other side and Karma is a super bitch. Don't go chasing waterfalls," I say smiling. "Oh shut up," he interrupts. "Don't you dare TLC me." We both laugh. We stare at each other for a while and then kissed each other so passionately that I could have sworn my panties almost came off. I walked him to the door and he said, "I love you homie" and put out his fist. "I love you too homie," I say and I touch my fist with his and close the door behind him. I took a shower, then got in the bed. What the hell just happened tonight? I just wanted to go out and dance.

Later that morning I received a text from Robyn.

Robyn: *Good morning Sunshine, brunch today?*

Me: *Yes please and thank you.*

Robyn: *Okay I'll be there in an hour.*

Me: *Perfect. I need a bellini ASAP.*

   I jump out the bed and start getting myself together. Today was definitely a no effort day. My hair was a curly mess. I had no intention of wearing any makeup. I was emotionally drained after last night's events. I just needed a happy drink. Robyn walks in my apartment and immediately starts telling me about her crazy weekend as I looked for shoes to wear. "So what's up Chica? You're so quiet. What's going on?" she asked. "Well I went out dancing with Naomi and when I came home my little world was flipped again," I say with a half smirk. "Wait what? What happened?" Robyn asked. As I tell Robyn the story, I can't keep count of how many times she said holy shit and then asked God to forgive her. "Wow, but wait what happened to DramaKing?" she asked. "I don't know I blocked him."

#

Chapter 8: The Hook Up...Introduction to StrawSipper

Time had passed and I felt better about the avoided clash of the titans with Superman and DramaKing. I couldn't believe that fool threw pebbles at my window. I really couldn't believe Superman considered leaving his fiancé. The idea of leaving someone for someone else never sat right with me. I feel if you're unhappy in a situation then you should ultimately do whatever it is that will make you happy. Hopping from one relationship to another increases the possibility of bringing baggage along with you. I think I can speak for those who have been able to move on and leave their baggage behind when I say, I did not spend all that time de-cluttering for someone else to come in my life and fill my good space up with their crap.

I decided to take a break from men and really just focus on myself. I literally ignored any guy that called or texted me that I used to date. I barely showed Superman any love and he's usually the exception. I thought maybe if I remained distant he would get married and forget all about me. Okay, maybe not forget ALL about me. That would be impossible, but certainly my distance would perhaps force him to remember why he got engaged in the first place. Maybe he could fall in love with his fiancé all over again. Truth be told, I would love for any guy that I've dated to be happy, move on with their lives, and most importantly, leave me the hell alone. I remember a guy friend from high school told me I throw people away. I thought that was a little harsh. I don't throw people away. I just stop speaking to people who I feel wronged me. Especially those who mistook my kindness for weakness. And don't get me started on the ones who were just plain jerks. Why should I give these people another opportunity to hurt me or try to break my spirit because they are unhappy with themselves? I can't continue to allow people to drain my energy and not replenish it. Allowing that behavior to continue is not good for your mental health.

It was a new day. I was on a path to new discoveries. Learning what I ...and then my phone rang, interrupting my train of thought. I answered and it was my mother. "Hello mother," I say annoyed that she interrupted my newly made affirmation. "Hello daughter! I have someone I think you should meet. There's a nice guy that just started working here on my job. Good looking guy. He's the new head of the tech department. He'll be perfect! Great benefits, 401k," she says. "Mom!" I interrupt. "No kids, 6ft tall like you like them. Why that is, I have no idea?" she continued. "Mom!" I interrupt again. "Good build, I mean he has a little bit of a belly, but nothing a few sit ups can't fix," she rambles. "MOM!" I scream. "Who are you screaming at like that?" she says in her stern voice. "Mom, I'm not interested. I need a break," I say, sounding exhausted.

"What you need is a date with a real man, a gentleman that knows how to treat a lady. You need someone who can pay the entire bill at a restaurant. Someone who wants you as girlfriend number 1 and only, and doesn't steal. Oh, and he won't need a ride anywhere because he has a car and won't take you to chain restaurants," she says sarcastically. "Okay those were a lot of shots fired. I feel like you're judging my taste in men," I say, giving the phone a side eye squint as I anticipate her response. "I'm not judging. I'm your mother. I would never judge you,. But I am slightly concerned about your ability to spot a jack ass when he throws the signs in your face. Every guy you have been out with in the past couple of years has been a mess. Let someone who knows you best, for example me, the woman who gave birth to you, hook you up with a nice guy. What's the harm in getting treated to dinner? If he's a jerk, well then, I'll apologize and mind my business. I'm 99 percent sure I would flip his desk over when I got to work. Nobody messes with my kids. If it works out I won't even say I told you so, but you do have to name your first born after me. Deal?" she asks proud of her proposition. "No Rumpelstiltskin, no deal. I'm not interested. I said no," I say, slightly annoyed at her persistence. "Okay fine. That's a very nasty attitude you have. You'll meet him at the job's annual yacht ride anyway. You might like him." "I seriously doubt it. You have no idea what I'm looking for." "WHAT! I said he was employed and tall!" she says laughing hysterically.

I hung up with my mother not sure how to feel. She totally had jokes on my dating life. Hell, now that I think about it, I had my own jokes. Maybe she was right. This would be something different. This guy could be a breath of fresh air. I'll make my decision after the yacht party. What am I going to wear?

I decided to head to my favorite department store Bloomingdales after work. Retail therapy always makes me feel better.

As I walk down Lexington Avenue there is just a sea of men in suits. Maybe I should have dressed up a little for this shopping trip. Focus Shaunie, you are looking for a dress to take home, not a man to take home. As I reach for the door this nice looking guy reaches for the door at the same time. He's about 6ft 2in with a handsome face. He could use a shave and his suit was a little too big, but he was undeniably cute. As he grabs the door handle he says, "You have such beautiful eyes Miss. Let me get that door for you." "Oh thank you," I say blushing. "I love your curls. I love when women wear their natural hair," "Oh really thank you again," I say, thinking to myself he has great teeth. "You got a dollar?" he asks. "Um wait what? Are you fucking kidding me? Ugh!" I say as I storm through the doors of my department store sanctuary.

As I look through the racks angrily, I realize that 1) I need to relax because I look crazy, and 2) I was in my happy place and distracted. I was probably missing amazing deals with all this angry dress searching. I take my phone out my pocket so I can find good shopping music and I see a text from Miranda. Miranda and I worked together at Job2. You know those people you just click with immediately? She went from co-worker to really great friend rather quickly. She's a little younger than me, but wise beyond her years, that's for sure. She's studying to be an actress and she is definitely ambitious enough to do it. She has a great head on her shoulders and my goodness she is hilarious. She always called me by these funny pet names.

Miranda: Hey Honey Bunches! How's your day going?

Me: Hey sunshine. It's going. I got duped by a homeless guy.

Miranda: Duped? Homeless guy? Hibiscus what are you talking about?

Me: Yeah he had on a suit and everything. He held the door for me. He threw compliments my way and then asked me for a dollar.

Miranda: LOL I am hysterically laughing outside in public. So I guess I just have one question.

Me: It's not funny he was cute and had nice teeth. Guess that explains why his suit was so big. What's the question?

Miranda: Did you give him the dollar? LOL

Me: LOL Oh you have jokes. Hell no I was pissed.

Miranda: OMG I can't breathe. What if he was coming from a job interview and needed bus fare home? LOL

Me: LOL What? You can't be serious. Why was hustle man so charming why?

Miranda: That's probably how he got the first dollar, using that charm and showing those pearly whites.

Me: LOL I'm so done with you.

Miranda: Okay, okay I'm sorry.

Me: So my mom is trying to hook me up with a gentleman suitor of her choosing.

Miranda: Uh Oh momma's on the case. Well at least we know he's employed. Is he tall? LOL

Me: Really Miranda Really? LOL I'm heading home. I'll text you later.

After a grueling train ride home, I was exhausted. I can't even begin to say how many times the train was held at the station delaying my commute home. I walk into my apartment determined to go the gym no matter what. I turned on the television in the living room and then went into my bedroom to hang my adorable yacht dress on the door. It was a little revealing, but fun and flirty. I put my gym clothes on and my phone rings. It was my mother. "Yes mom" I say. "What's up kiddo? I wanted to know if you found something to wear for tomorrow; also if you're going to drive. The job has free reserved parking," she says. "Yes I found something today. Oh and I got hit on." "Of course you did honey. You're so cute. You look just like your mother. Was he tall?" she asks jokingly. "He was tall with pretty teeth. It was going well until he asked me for a dollar!" I say laughing. "Wait what? Did you give him the dollar?" she asks laughing hysterically. "No why does everyone keep asking that? Anyway my dress is cute and I am driving. I'm going to leave work a little early so I can come home and change." "Okay honey bunny. I'm about to watch 'Scandal' so I'll see you tomorrow. Later gator!" she says.

I hung up with my mom still focused. I was going to the gym that night. I heard the intro to *Scandal* on the television, and instead of filling my water bottle with water I ended up filling a wine glass with wine. I made myself a little fruit and cheese plate and yes you guessed it, sat on the couch and watched the show in my gym clothes. "I'll work out in the morning," I told myself. Cheers to Olivia Pope!

I wake up in the morning energized. I looked at the clock and it was 7am. I forgot to set my alarm for an earlier time. No time to exercise this morning oh well. Tomorrow is another day.

I did manage to grab a yogurt out the fridge before I rush out the door. I've been protesting buying breakfast ever since BagelBoy ruined it. I was happy I remembered the yogurt. Good breakfast spots were hard to come by. Everyone doesn't sprinkle powdered sugar on their French toast. Once again confirming to myself why I need to be on strike from men. They ruin stuff.

I get to work and Sasha has left me a voicemail message: "Call me as soon as you get to your desk." Oh this has to be good. "Good morning Sasha darling. Dish the dirt," I say. She begins to tell me the story of yet another mailroom clerk who was fired for stupidity. Apparently this one was caught stealing, on-camera. I swear that mailroom has a revolving door. I refuse to learn anyone else's name unless they have been there for more than one year. "She wasn't very friendly so, oh well," I say, ready to move on to a more pressing topic…the boat. "So listen. The yacht ride for my mom's job is tonight. I get to meet the guy she's been pushing for the past week." "Well at least you know he's employed. Is he tall?" Sasha asks. "Seriously, why does everyone keep asking that? Am I that shallow? Do I emphasize tall that much? There are so many other qualities that are just as important. Trustworthy, dependable..," I say. "Yeah okay love that's great, but how tall is he?" Sasha interrupts. "6ft!" "Yes! You can wear your stilettos and still look up at him. Be nice to him. I hope he doesn't say anything stupid. Your mother would go back to the office and flip his desk over," Sasha says laughing. "You know entirely too much about my life," I say. "You know

137

I'm like family. Let me answer these phones. Bye Chica," Sasha says. Another mail room person bites the dust. This has to be the 5th one in the past 3 months. Ridiculous.

The day is going by and I'm starving. I was trying not to eat too much since I would be indulging in food and drinks on the boat later. My stomach growls were too loud to ignore so I decided to run outside and buy a bag of popcorn and a Snickers as back up. As I turn the corner I hear "Well, well, well there goes my Boo! She's always rushing right into my arms." Oh no. "Hello BagelBoy. How's your Connecticut girlfriend?" I ask sarcastically. "She's good, but I miss you though. You're really not going to give me a hug?" he asks, making a pout face. "Hell no I am not. You're already taking up too much of my time good bye," I say as I turn away abruptly and begin walking with my head held high. "You have a boyfriend yet?" he yells. "NO!" I yell. Damn, damn, damn why did I answer that fool? "That was a trick question girl. I'm right here. You know you miss me!" he yells. "Good bye BagelBoy!" I yell back and enter the store to get my snacks. He's such a charming arrogant jackass ugh. Where the hell is the pop…ooh Doritos!

4pm finally rolled around and I head home. I can't lie, I was actually excited to meet this guy. Maybe it was my curiosity. My mom wouldn't steer me wrong right? After all she gave birth to me as she loves to remind me. I get home and immediately start rushing to get ready. The dress was a little more revealing than I thought. The girls were really on display. A lady has to leave something to the imagination right? I knew I would need a lot of safety pins for this ensemble. I pinned the dress where I could so the girls wouldn't pop out during the Cha Cha Slide. I fluff up my curls and take one last look in the mirror. I totally have to wear this outfit again when I go out with Robyn and Naomi. This is cute. Go hard or go home Shaunie. Cheers to the freaking weekend!

I park the car in the reserved area. Mom, Auntie, and I proceed to board the boat. It was rocking a little from the waves and they were giving drinks to the passengers as we boarded, so cute. "So they want us to maintain our balance as we walk in heels on the shaky boat with our bag in one hand and drink in the other? You know I get those heel spurs," Auntie whispers to me. "It looks that way!" I say giggling. "Well, all righty then! Let's go Boo. I'll take the sangria. Cheers!" Auntie says as she tucks her purse under her arm and takes the glass of sangria. I followed suit. We look for a table in the back. We always have the fun table no matter where we go, so we have to plan strategically. "Look Shaunie they have a photo booth, AWW yeah you know where we'll be," Auntie says as we clink glasses. We love taking pictures, especially Auntie. She may not know how to use all the functions on her smart phone, but she sure knows how to get the right lighting on that camera. "I see it. There's a table in the corner by the window let's go!" Mom says as she charged toward the back. As we sit down, we clink glasses and say cheers for making it to our seats without falling or spilling our drinks. It's always important to celebrate even the small victories in life. As we're laughing and chatting away, more people get on the yacht and more people want to sit at our table. I guess they could sense a good time vibe with us.

I get up to get us another round of sangria and I hear. "Hey StrawSipper, how are you? Shaunie, Shaunie this is StrawSipper. he's our new tech guy," Mom says. As I shake StrawSipper's hand my mom is behind him giving me this wide-eyed stare and pumping two thumbs up. I try not to laugh because my Auntie is doing the same face, but instead of the thumbs up, she's pretending to clap her hands. "Hello StrawSipper. It's very nice to meet you. Did you come straight from work or is there a body in that big bag you're holding?" I ask trying to be charming with a side of asshole. "It's very nice to meet you too Shaunie. Yes I just came from work. There's no body in here just the head!" he says and we both laugh. Well I've heard that when you dish out sarcasm, if the person responds with sarcasm instead of getting offended, he's a keeper. He was actually nice-looking. He favored Morris Chestnut to me. Smooth chocolate complexion. Fresh haircut, button-up shirt, slacks, and well- buffed shoes. It was clear he took good care of himself. If he smells good he may have a real shot. "Ladies this is my older brother Dreadlocks," StrawSipper says. As Dreadlocks waves we all say in unison, "HI BROTHER DREADLOCKS!" We giggled and clinked empty glasses celebrating our unplanned unison greeting. "What are you ladies drinking?" Dreadlocks asked. We all raised our glasses and said, "SANGRIA!" StrawSipper and Dreadlocks laughed and shook their heads. "Then Sangria it is. We'll have someone come over," StrawSipper says as he walked away.

"So that's him huh. Not bad kiddo. Good job Patty Cakes," Auntie says to me and mom. My mom's name is Patricia, but for as long as I can remember, Auntie always called her Patty Cakes. "See I told you. He's nice looking right? He's employed and bonus he's tall," Mom says trying to literally pat herself on the back. "He's nice looking and kind of funny. We'll see, don't get your hopes up," I say as I sip the last drop of sangria in my glass. "That Dreadlocks guy is pretty cute too. I wonder if he's... well hello gentleman. Welcome baaaaack!" Auntie sings slightly. She was hoping they didn't hear the beginning of her comment. "Cheers ladies! Here's to having a good time and being in great company!" StrawSipper says as he looks at me and we all toast.

The music is going and the drinks are flowing. Laughter filled the yacht. It didn't feel like a work event even though we all remained on our best behavior. It was time to go to the lower level where dinner was being served. We decided to take a few pictures at the photo booth since it was on the way. "Look Shaunie they have props. I'm so excited!" Auntie says with a huge grin on her face. "And there's no one working the booth. You just push the button and start posing. It is so on!" I say, extremely excited. Mom, Auntie and I have at it. I can't tell you how many times we pushed the button for our extensive photo shoot. Finally my mom's boss says, "Look at these hams! Get your butts downstairs so we can all eat together. You all have me rushing up these stairs because people are looking for you three. You almost made me spill my sangria." All three of our faces

141

pouted. We put our heads down and said "Sorry" like 3 big kids. We took our time walking carefully behind boss lady down the stairs. Everyone knows sangria and stilettos don't always mix.

We sit down in our saved seats at the fun table and StrawSipper is sitting directly across from me. The food is yummy and the glasses are still clinking. StrawSipper and Dreadlocks were telling us jokes about their family and making funny movie references. We were totally feeding off of each other's energy and then it happened. The song everyone had been waiting for. "Come on everybody. Get out your seats and join me on the dance floor for the Cha Cha Slide" the DJ yells into the microphone. The DJ restarted the song 5 times before he let it play in its entirety. Our entire table bolted to the dance floor. "Let's see what you got pretty lady!" StrawSipper says to me as he does some weird foot shuffle and claps his hands to the beat. "I know dance moves to videos Hun. Aaliyah's 'Are You That Somebody,' Janet's 'I Get So Lonely.' I can Cha Cha Slide with my eyes closed," I say confidently. "Please don't. I want to see those beautiful eyes of yours and more importantly I don't want you injuring any of my co-workers," StrawSipper says and we both start laughing and dance the night away. While we are all enjoying ourselves I notice Auntie and Dreadlocks having the time of their lives. I see her blushing and giggling as he twirls her around the dance floor. I guess she forget all about those heel spurs. Auntie was showing off her smooth moves completely unbothered.

The Captain made an announcement that we would be reporting back to the dock in 30 minutes. I look across the room and lock eyes with Auntie. We were so in sync. It was photo booth time. This time we invited the table to join us for our rapid picture-taking. My mom's co-workers were asking to take pictures with us. We were getting asked a lot. It was like we became the props. We must have taken over 20 pictures. We get back to the dock and it's time to part ways when Dreadlocks says, "Hey let's go to a lounge!" StrawSipper chimes in with, "Yeah let's keep the party going!" I look at Mom and Auntie and they looked like they were fine to go or not go. They completely left the decision up to me. "Let's lounge it up!" I say and everyone cheered. Guess I made the right choice.

We get to the lounge and it's kind of empty. It was a little after 9 on a Friday night. The crowd doesn't really get going until about 11pm. We find a booth and kind of make it our own VIP Section. StrawSipper and Dreadlocks went to get us drinks and Mom and Auntie were bopping really hard to the music. You could tell they haven't been to a club in a while. Mom leans in and says, "It's cute in here, but it's so loud. Why is it so loud?" While Auntie is dancing in her seat and snapping her fingers, she says to mom, "Oh stop it Patty Cakes. You're being old." I just sat there and laughed at myself. I would have never thought I would be sitting in a club waiting for drinks with my mother and aunt. I'm so happy they don't look their age. People always think we're sisters.

The guys return with our drinks and the DJ starts playing 90's Hip Hop and R&B. It was like he had my IPod. I think the

143

DJ played everything from the Bad Boy era: Faith, Mase, Biggie, the list went on and on as I did my little two-step, sipped my drink, and sung every word. Then he played Beyoncé and it was like I transformed. I had to put my drink down. The dance floor was now my stage and I had to give the people what they wanted or, well, give the people what they didn't know they wanted. I forgot how bad my feet hurt as I danced circles around StrawSipper. I commended him for trying to keep up. After my Beyoncé / Destiny's Child performance I decided to sit down and rest. Plus I was beginning to sweat and that is not cute outside of the gym.

StrawSipper stands in front of me and tells me how he would like to call me and take me out some time. Did I mention my mom was sitting right next to me? I was intrigued by his bravery to go in for the kill as my mom swayed back and forth singing Terror Squad's "Lean Back." "Um excuse me young lady. Where is your sister while you're doing all this lean back dancing?" I say to my mom who is clearly in a zone. "Um she's over there in that booth with Dreadlocks. She's getting her groove back. Go Stella Go!" she cheered. StrawSipper and I laughed. "I think it's time I took the kiddies to bed," I say to StrawSipper. "Oh is it past their bedtime?" StrawSipper asks laughing. "Yes absolutely. I have one making out in the corner and if the other one leans back any further she's going to lean over. Thank you so much for a lovely time. We'll text and set up a day for us to get together," I say quite professionally for some reason. "Thank you ever so much Ms. Shaunie. I look forward to speaking to you at a later date," StrawSipper says and we both start laughing. "Oh well, well, well look who came up for air. Welcome baaaaack!" I sing as Auntie and Dreadlocks walked toward us. They looked like two love-struck teenagers, holding hands and giggling. It was actually quite adorable. "Let's hit it Stella! Glad your groove is back, but it's time to go home!" Mom says as she stretches her hands out and StrawSipper pulls her up off the seat. Hmm, point for StrawSipper. He's a total gentleman. The guys walk us to my car and everyone hugs goodnight. Auntie and Dreadlocks's hug was a lot longer than everyone else's. Something was brewing there. Maybe there would be two love connections from this meet and greet. Time would certainly tell.

#

Chapter 9: The Hook Up...My date with StrawSipper

"So how's it going with StrawSipper?" Robyn asks as we rate clutch bags with our thumbs up or thumbs down scoring system. We decided to check out Saks Fifth Avenue's outlet store in New Jersey early Saturday morning before too many people arrive and ruin the experience. I look forward to the day I can shop in a store opened early just for me. "It's going. He makes me laugh and he's a talker which is a good thing I suppose," I say as I thumbs down this boring brown clutch Robyn was holding. "That's a great thing he's a talker. If he only texted you, you two would get nowhere. When is your date again? Seriously thumbs down for this clutch? Look, one side is leather, the other side is calf hair!" Robyn says, demanding a recount.

"Oh okay. You didn't show me the other side. I like it now. Hold on to that. I suppose you're right about the talking. Talking is a forgotten form of communication. Everything is text and email these days. You can be in a room full of people and everyone's head is down because they are doing something on their phones. Like hello people! I thought this was a dinner party." I stop talking and look at Robyn who is diligently typing on her phone. I cleared my throat loudly. Robyn looks up and says, "What I'm totally listening. He invited you to a dinner party continue!" I give her a side eye squint and continue.

"He's taking me out next Sunday for brunch. Here's something interesting. He sends me a lot of art work with naked black couples embracing. Ooh this is cute, look at this!" I say excited, holding up a bright leather turquoise clutch with black studs around the edge. Robyn laughs out loud and says, "He sent you what? Ooh that bag is cute. Hold on to that. Why is he sending you pictures of random naked people?" "Okay stop, don't do that. I'm trying to be mature here. It's not random naked people. They are posing. It's that erotica art like Janet Jackson on the cover of 'Rolling Stone' when her hubby was holding the girls for her," I explain. "Oh it's famous people? Where the hell did he get those?" Robyn asks. "No I said it's like that, except these are unknowns and they are wearing tribal king and queen crown things with feathers and warrior paint," I say trying to keep a straight face. Meanwhile Robyn is staring at me with her eyes beginning to tear. You know when you're trying to stop coughing so you try to hold it in, but the coughs keep coming? Well that's how she looked trying to contain her laughter. She then turns away, hides in a rack of fur vests, and bursts into laughter. I on the other hand remained composed and continued to find clutch bags on the shelf as if everyone receives pictures of warrior royalty hugging on their phones daily.

"Shaunie you are killing me right now. How did he even feel comfortable showing you stuff like that?" Robyn asked. "Well we were on the phone for a little over an hour and I asked him if he had Instagram. He said he used to, but his account kept getting deleted so he stopped using it. When I asked why, he said he guessed the pictures he posted weren't PG enough." "And of course your curious butt said, 'Oh yeah like what? Let me see.' Am I right? Go on, tell me I'm right," Robyn says mocking me. I simply walked up to her with my nose in the air, snatched that brown clutch out her hand and screamed, "You don't know my life!" and threw the clutch in a bin of silk scarfs. Robyn could not stop laughing. "Oh my stomach hurts. Why do you make me laugh like this? So after he sent the picture what did you say?" Robyn asked. "I said oh wow! Okay yeah! Look at that! That's interesting! He asked if I liked art like that and I said it's cool it's different. Then the next thing I know he sent me like 5 in a row." I say innocently. "Look at this come get close." I show Robyn the texted pictures. "Oh, oh, oh my, wait you weren't kidding about the feathers! "Well look at it this way. He could be a real passionate lover. He may be able to do lifts!" she says with a wink. "Oh my word woman, you're so nasty. What is Blake doing to you?" I say teasing her about her new boyfriend. "Everything!" Robyn says with a huge grin on her face. I give her a high five. "Aren't we supposed to be looking for his birthday gift?" I ask Robyn as she stares at me holding three clutch bags, a bottle of perfume, and a silk scarf. "Yep!" as we stood there staring at each other, laughing as she balanced all of her merchandise in her arms. As we head to the register Robyn asked, "Wait, you said Brunch on Sunday. What happened to the dinner party?" I just shook my head.

Sunday finally arrived and I couldn't believe I was slightly nervous. StrawSipper and I had been speaking every day for the past two weeks. It felt natural and a little weird all at the same time. Maybe it was because my Mom initiated this premature union. I fought with myself all week about what would be a good first brunch date outfit. I decided to wear a tangerine silk wrap dress, big gold hoops and gold sandals. I made sure my hair was big, curly and fluffy. My cat eye makeup was gentle yet fierce. I sprayed myself with so much perfume I coughed. I agreed to let him pick me up at my apartment at 2pm. It was 1:55pm when he texted me he was outside. I grabbed my clutch and headed downstairs.

I walk out the door and he's standing there with flowers and a heart shaped box of chocolates. Wow what a gentleman. "Hello gorgeous!" he says. "Hello handsome, is all this for me?" I ask as he gives an awkward hug because he's holding all my gifts in his hands. "I hope you like flowers because if you don't I'm going to need you to pretend just a little while longer. I'm sensitive!" he says trying to keep a straight face as he opens the car door. I smile and wait for him to get in before I answer. He gets in and looks at me. "I love flowers and and..." I say as I'm examining the box of chocolates. "Monsters Inc. chocolate candies from Valentine's Day? Did you re-gift? When do these expire?" I ask laughing. "See, see what had happened was. First off they haven't expired I checked. They were sitting in my refrigerator because I was supposed to give them to my mom and well, I kept forgetting to take them with me when I visit her on Sundays. You're going to tell your mom I bought you some stale-ass candy aren't you?" he asked laughing. With a straight face I looked him in the eyeballs and said, "Yes!" Then I turned away

149

and put on my seat belt trying my hardest not to laugh. "You are something else. This brunch is going to be fun!" he replied.

He took me to a really nice brunch place in Harlem. I've never been to Billie's Black before so he was happy that he was the first to bring me there. It's a great restaurant, one of Harlem's gems. I ordered the salmon cakes and waffles. He ordered crab cakes and waffles. Little did he know he just kissed our goodbye kiss goodbye. I guess he forgot I was allergic to shellfish. The restaurant offered unlimited bellinis so I did not limit myself. The owner of the restaurant kept coming over asking if everything was okay and if we were enjoying ourselves. I thought that was very nice. Then he came over with two complimentary shots of his fruit-infused vodka. He said we made a beautiful couple and StrawSipper better not mess it up. I said cheers to that and all three of us clinked shot glasses and threw them back. We were having such a great time. StrawSipper asks, "So shall we keep this party going? Do you have time for a movie?" "Sure let's go! What's out?" I ask extremely excited. "I'm not sure let's just go and see what happens." Spontaneous…I like it.

We get to the theater and the movie didn't start for another hour. Luckily there was a cute restaurant inside the theater where people could wait and have a drink before their movie started. We sit at the bar and I ordered a raspberry mojito and he ordered a Blue Moon. As he sips his beer through a straw I can't help but wonder why this is happening. "Why are you drinking beer with a straw?" I ask. "Because it comes with one, duh!" he says quickly. I liked that my sarcasm did not faze him one bit.

The night was ending and I have to say, shockingly, I'd had a really nice time. He got out of the car, opened my door for me, and walked me to my building. We said we would see each other in a week or so (I had events coming up plus my overnight job and he had his own obligations). Neither one of us wanted to put the pressure on the other. We gave each other a long hug and I gave him a kiss on the cheek. That's all he could get, since he ate the crab cakes earlier. We called it a night and I went upstairs. I could not wait to get out of these heels. I sat on the couch with my flowers and my old chocolate and thought of my mom's proposition. I can't believe I may have to name my first born Patty Cakes. I'm never going to hear the end of this.

As the weeks went on I started to notice that StrawSipper was taking a long time to ask me on another date. When I suggested days to go out, he would say they didn't work for him. Then he would suggest walks in the park and grabbing a hot dog. I would decline because well EWW and it was getting cold outside. If you end up having a stroll in the park that's one thing, its sweet it may even be romantic, but to just go to the park and start strolling? Who the hell does that on purpose? Then it hit me. Was he blowing me off? Did I have too many bellinis? Maybe funds were low and it wasn't a pay week. Plus he hadn't been on the job that long. Maybe he was adjusting to his new finances. So I went back and forth with this in my mind for a couple of days. He was certainly reaching out to me every day so he obviously liked me. I can't even count how many of these tribal sexy pictures I had in my phone at this point. I must like him. I mean I got past the fact that he had a roommate and he was in his thirties. Living in New York alone is expensive. Trust me I know. I live it every day. Perhaps he was saving to get his own place and money was tight. I needed advice and I needed it fast. So I called the two women that were there from the beginning, my mom and aunt.

"Hello ladies, it appears I am in a pickle and need your honest opinion," I say. "What's up buttercup?" Mom says. "A pickle you say. Oh my. Go on," Auntie says. "Well StrawSipper did such a great job on the first date and now I'm feeling like he's flaking on the second date. I speak to him every day so I imagine if he wasn't interested I wouldn't hear from him as much, right?" I ask innocently. "Maybe his money is funny and he doesn't want you to know," Mom says. "Some men don't share their financial struggles. Pride and ego play a big factor," Auntie says. "But he went all out for the first date. Why spend like that if you didn't have it like that?" I ask confused. "He was trying to impress you!" Mom and Auntie say at the same time. They were tickled that they were so in sync with each other. "Okay, okay settle down. What I'm about to say goes against all my rules. Maybe I should...can't believe I'm about to say this. Maybe I should offer to...oh man why is this so hard?" I say. "PAY!" Auntie says. "Oh God I feel sick. It's very hot in here. Are you hot? Oh boy!" I say breathing heavily. "Oh stop it. It's not a bad thing. If you really like him it's not that big of a deal," Mom says. "Think of it as a fun outing and not a date. You don't have to treat him to a 5 star restaurant. I treated Dreadlocks to coffee and I feel good about it," Auntie says. "Yes okay, but how many dates have you two gone on since the boat?" I ask. "Oh like 5!" Auntie says with a girly giggle. "You see. This is only date two. My money shouldn't exist until we are in a committed relationship," I whine. "What? Girl you know you need to stop. Give it a try. He's a nice guy and you obviously like him," Mom says. "Go to Applebee's and get a 2 for $20!" Auntie says teasing me. "Good one sis!" Mom says laughing. I take a deep breath and say, "Okay, okay I will do it. What happened to being courted huh? What happened to the days when a guy wooed you and just showered you with gifts." "That will happen for you sunshine. Listen, a real man is going to give you the world because a woman that asks for nothing deserves everything. Got it?" Auntie says. "That's right, so get your independent butt off the phone and treat the man to a chicken wing," Mom says and we all start laughing. I hung up and made the call.

"Hi StrawSipper, how was your day?" I ask. "Better now. How are you gorgeous?" he says. "I'm good. Listen, I was thinking we could go to Buffalo Wild Wings and watch the game. My treat! What do you say?" "Wow um yeah okay. Listen just because you're treating doesn't mean I'm putting out." he says. "We'll see about that. You're driving though." I say laughing. "Cool. I can pick you up at 8. Does that work?" he asks. "Yes 8 works great." "She's treating and she's a rapper. Nice!" he says laughing. I hung up with him and felt okay about my decision.

153

I decided I would not get all dolled up like the first date. I was simply treating a buddy to a light dinner. Stilettos were not required for appetizers and beer. He picked me up and we were off. We were laughing as usual and shared stories about our day during the car ride. The restaurant was crowded and the wait was like 30 minutes. I was starving and in no mood to wait so I suggested he go in the open seating area and grab an empty table. He ran with my suggestion and we were successful. We sat and the waitress came over right away. StrawSipper asked what kind of beer she recommended for the season and of course she mentions pumpkin ale. He was feeling adventurous so he ordered it. He was trying something new. When the waitress asked if he wanted a regular size or a large, he paused for a second before saying, "Bring on the large. Go hard or go home right." Oh no, he didn't! Woosaaa Shaunie. Just smile and nod, smile and nod.

As I focused on smiling and nodding the waitress says, "Miss, miss." I did not hear her ask me what I wanted to drink. I apparently had zoned out. "I'm sorry long day. I'll have a cider thank you!". "We only have Angry Orchard is that okay?" she asked. "Yes that's perfect thank you," the waitress walks away. "So what kind of wings should we get?" I ask. "Boneless for sure, but I'm stuck on the flavors. I have a little bit of a cold so I can't taste much," he says. "Well my favorite is Mango Habanero. It's sweet, but has a real kick. Do you like spicy?" "Um yeah that's cool. I'll try anything once," he says winking. I truly hate that statement, especially when guys say it. I don't know why; it just makes me think of perverted things and I'm immediately questioning their sexual conquests.

The waitress comes over with the drinks and boy oh boy is that beer large. It's huge. She gives me my cider in the bottle. "We are going to have the Mango Habanero boneless wings," I say. "What size?" she asks. He looks at me and shrugs his shoulders. "Large. Go hard or go home right?" I say and he gives me a high five. "Um excuse me. Can we do half mango half lemon pepper seasoning? I'm sorry that just seems like a lot of spicy," StrawSipper says to the waitress. She smiles, says no problem, and takes our menus. I just stare at him taken aback that he changed the order. "I hope you don't mind," he says. "Lemon pepper is a dry rub. EWW. We totally should have discussed this play coach before we got on the field. It's all good," I say teasing.

"Cheers to our second um outing um with just the two of us," I say. We clink bottle to glass and I take a swig. He pauses and says "AWW man I need a straw. She didn't leave a straw." "What? It's a beer. They don't give you a straw for a beer," I say laughing and take another swig of my cider. "No I just need a straw. Stop looking at me like that. Listen I have a cold and let's say I drink out of this glass. They may not properly wash the glass. Stay with me on this. The next person to drink off this glass may run the risk of getting my cold hence I need a straw to stop the passing of the germs. Why are you looking at me like that?" he asks, still looking for the waitress. I can't say how I was looking at him, but I can certainly tell you what I was thinking. Are you fucking kidding me? "WHAT! You're joking right?" I ask laughing. "No," he says. "I'm so serious. I need a straw. I can't drink this without it." I waved the waitress over and asked her for a straw. She looked at my bottle and looked at me puzzled. I said, "Not for me for him. He has a cold and doesn't want to spread his germs." The waitress's puzzled look did not leave her face as she said okay and walked away to get the straw.

The food came and he couldn't handle the heat of the mango habanero. The poor man's nose started running. I felt like I was doing my part in helping him get rid of his cold. He gulped massive amounts of beer through that straw trying to cool his mouth. The waitress came back and asked if we wanted a second round of drinks and he says, "Yeah let's keep the party going!" Oh no he didn't! Well look who's comfortable with me paying. You're not even my boyfriend yet. Okay Shaunie calm down. You're overreacting. He's having a good time. I know he better not try for a third round because the party won't be going anywhere. He was certainly trying to make me laugh all night with his impressions and movie trivia. After a while I was a little annoyed at the lack of real conversation. When the bill came he automatically reached for it. I told him if he opened it, he would have to pay it. He placed the bill down on the table and slid it over to me. Wow this transaction was really about to happen. As I look over the bill and snarl at the 2 large beers and I go in my bag to get my debit card. This bill wasn't bad at all. It was under $60. As I sign the merchants copy he says, "I think it's sexy when a woman pays." Then he sips some more beer through that freaking straw. I smiled and went to the rest room. When I came back he was fully engaged in a conversation with these two guys that was sitting next to us. He was standing there with his glass, sipping his beer cracking jokes about the players on the team. I liked that he was a social butterfly, but I was ready to go. I walked up and started laughing along with them. "I'm ready," I said, with the only straight face.

While walking to the car he decides to tell me of his plans to move to Atlanta and build a house. He wanted to have a ton of kids and he felt like he would have a better life in the south. He was really trying to convince me of how great it would be out there because the cost of living was cheaper. I wouldn't take the bait. I had already been through this with Vegas. Maybe I would consider Connecticut or even Jersey, well maybe not Jersey, but the south was totally out of the question. "I made it in New York. I'm ready to leave and make it somewhere else. It's easier in the south." He continued talking and my mind drifted. You ever hear somebody say something so stupid it made you squint? How could he have possibly made it in New York when I just paid for dinner and he has a roommate? His choice of words was all wrong. He definitely needed to rephrase. I haven't made it in New York yet, but I'll be damned if I give up and move just because it's easier. I've always been taught to fight for what I want. All I kept envisioning was me living in Atlanta with him and our six kids. We're all sitting down for breakfast and no one would drink their milk because I forgot to put the straws on the table. "Why are you looking at me like that?" he asked. I'm sure my look was one of confusion. "I'm not moving to Atlanta ever.

157

I don't care how big the house is. I never grew up in a house so that's not a big deal for me. I want a penthouse anyway and a stingy car. All white BMW with two seats to be exact. I want all that here in New York. I'm a New Yorker and I'm not leaving." I finished my I love New York speech and opened the car door myself. I was ready to go.

In the car he played a lot of 90's R&B: Hi Five, New Edition, and Tevin Campbell. The list goes on. I sang my little heart out. I didn't care about impressing him. I didn't care what he thought of my singing. I was being myself. We sat in the car for a little while longer after he pulled up to my building and he turned into a 90's music DJ. It was great. He played one hit after the other and we sang every song together. About an hour later I got out the car. I kind of liked him again. He walked me to the door and we hugged. He held my waist for a while and I said, "So are you going to kiss me?" He laughed and went for it. I felt nothing. Maybe I was thinking too much. Not a butterfly, not a spark, not a tingle. It was at that moment I decided he wasn't my kind of guy. He's a great catch, don't get me wrong, but there was something missing that I can't explain. I became distant and he eventually got the hint. It's not like I was going to run into him again right? Wrong. Auntie and Dreadlocks became a couple. Although our run-ins would be few and far between, there was no doubt that a run-in would occur every now and again. Good thing we're mature adults because if he was a jerk I would have thrown straws at him every time I saw him. He's a nice guy and I'm sure he would make the right woman very happy, but the chemistry wasn't there for me and I wasn't into wasting other people's time. I never should have abandoned my dating hiatus before I was ready. Always trust your gut.

#

Chapter 10: A New Year & Online Dating Again: Chef OnALedge & Dr. NoNotReally

"Regrets are a waste of time. They're the past crippling you in the present."[5] I find myself reciting this quote quite often lately. It's actually a line from one of my favorite movies *Under the Tuscan Sun*. After watching it I fantasize about vacationing in Europe. I imagine loving it so much I would just stay and build a life there. Perhaps live in London, maybe be a writer and be inspired by taking walks in the rain. I would wear a really cute trench coat while holding up my unbreakable umbrella and not care about my frizzy curls as I rush inside of a café for a spot of tea. Ah the thought of a sweet escape is so comforting when life keeps throwing curveballs your way.

With each relationship or guy I've dated, I've learned something. As weird as it may sound, I've learned more about myself. Haven't really pinpointed what I want, but I definitely know what I don't want. So I guess that's a start. I was definitely making some changes and I had every intention of leaving the past in the past. At the end of the day, I've had experiences that have made me stronger. My new plan is to continue to grow, be better, and improve. Worrying about what should have, could have, or would have been is not going to help me become my best me. So with that said, bring on the New Year. Mama needs a fresh start.

It was the morning of New Year's Eve and my friends and I still had no plans in the works (go figure). All Robyn knew for sure was she was going to church and was down for the shenanigans when she got out. Naomi and Le Boyfriend decided to be old farts and stay home. Victoria invited me over to her house, but I declined. Last year, Jada and I went to Victoria and her hubby's New Year's Eve game night and to our surprise it was couple central. She said there would be a lot of couples, but she didn't say only couples. The guys of course were friendly. They were introducing themselves and learning our names while their counter parts gave us the side eye and snarled at their friendly men. We did our best to make the ladies comfortable with small talk because Lord knows we had no interest in their other halves. After a few drinks and games everyone loosened up a bit and it turned out to be a nice evening.

This year was going to be different. I was going to celebrate loud with bubbly, watch the ball drop, and possibly kiss a tall, dark, and handsome man with fresh breath and life goals. Raquel invited me to her house earlier in the day. We were going to get dressed up and go out. Since she lived near Union Square, we could walk to a local bar lounge to bring in the New Year and then go back to her place to crash. I had planned to keep Robyn posted with my whereabouts so she knew where to meet me. As I'm getting my outfit together, I get a text from Superman.

Superman: *Hello*

Me: *Hey Sunshine what's up?*

Superman: *Nothing I'm outside. I'm free roaming in these streets. LOL Wanted to know if it was okay to stop by.*

Me: *Okay sure.*

Superman: *Cool be there in 30 minutes.*

The last time we saw each other was during the clash of the titans run-in at my apartment. So although we remained friends it still wasn't the same. At least I didn't feel it was the same. It had been months since we saw each other and our texts were very generic. It's weird. We know we can never be together in this lifetime, but we still feel the need to be around somehow, no matter how small the part we play in each other's lives. I bought him some cologne as a kind of gag gift. We kept seeing this advertisement for it when we went on our first road trip a couple of years back. I figured we could laugh about it even if it stunk.

Superman arrived in 30 minutes just as he said he would and I had all the stuff I was taking to Raquel's laid out ready to go. I had to be clear that I was on my way out and this visit would be short. "Hello," he says as he walks through the door toward the living room. "Hello" I say as I watched him walk. He always had a great walk. It was smooth and confident. Very Denzel-like. He knew I was watching him. This was a total set-up. This man will not get the best of me this New Year's Eve. I had plans for the night and plans for the New Year and neither involved his charming, smooth-walking ass.

"I was surprised to hear from you, especially tonight.

What are you doing in these streets?" I ask laughing. "Well I'm actually headed to my boy Gerard's house. He's having a little something. I figured since I was out I could check on you. See how you were doing," he says with a smile. He's such a charmer this guy. "Oh okay, well I'm actually heading out soon so…" I say as I look over to all of the stuff I needed to pack for Raquel's. "Oh it's cool. I don't want to keep you. I just wanted to see you before the year ended and give you your gift," he says digging in his pocket. As he's pulling out the gift I think to myself: Woo Hoo he bought me a gift. I was totally prepared to give him his gift whether I got one in return or not. I practiced my "oh it's okay don't worry about it. I wasn't expecting a gift anyway" face after I received his text saying he was coming. So I was prepared to give my Oscar-worthy performance in case he didn't deliver.

"Oh wow! You got me a gift. I wasn't sure we were doing that this year," I say smiling reaching for the box. "Yeah I wasn't going to skip this year. We went through a lot, but you're my friend right?" he asks with his fist out waiting for me to connect my fist with his. We bumped fists and I took a minute and just looked at him. He was giving me the face I had practiced earlier. It was clear to me that he didn't think I had a gift for him. I laughed to myself and got up to go get his gift. "I wasn't going to skip this year either," I said handing over the box. "Oh wow, for me? You are something else you know that," he says with a big smile on his face. "You didn't have to get me anything. Girl you crazy," as he starts ripping his gift open. We both were laughing because we looked like big kids trying to undo the fancy wrapping on our gifts. "Are you serious?" he says laughing. "This is hilarious, thank you.". "I thought you would get a kick out of that. Open it! I want to know how it smells." His smile was genuine as he opened the box. I could tell he really appreciated the gift. He sprayed it in the air and we both leaned in to catch a whiff. We looked at each other with our eyes wide open. We were in complete shock. The cologne actually smelled really good. I get so much joy out of giving gifts, especially when the person appreciates the thought behind it.

"Wow this smells good. I like it. Thank you. Okay your turn. I hope you like it," he said patiently waiting for me to open my box. I could not believe my eyes. It was a sun Pandora charm. It had yellow enamel and a smiley face. I jumped up and gave him the biggest, tightest hug. "I love it thank you so much. I can't believe you bought this for me," I say, just staring at the charm in AWE. "You're sunshine!" he said smiling. I hugged him again, then ran into my bedroom to get my bracelet. For years I've complained that even though I had this bracelet, people always struggle with what to buy me. A charm is the easiest thing. The gift showed me that Superman actually listens to me when I'm rambling. He yet again proved that he totally gets me. Simple things can be priceless treasures. He knows me well.

I added the charm to my bracelet and decided to wear it that evening. "What time are you trying to get to Gerard's?" I ask. "I have time, well I mean, unless you want me to leave now. What time did you plan on leaving?" he asked, taken aback by my abruptness. "I'm leaving in a few minutes. I want to give myself time, just in case I get stuck in traffic," I say putting on my boots. "Oh okay. Well just kick me out. It's all good. I don't want to keep you playa," he said jokingly. I wasn't trying to be rude. I just know us. We exchanged sentimental gifts, he smelled amazing, had a fresh haircut, clothes fit him perfect, and we were sharing too many googly-eye stares. It was time for him to leave. The panties were going to drop at any moment. We've come too far to turn back now.

"Okay cool. Thank you so much for coming. It was nice seeing you before the year ended," I say, passing him his hat and scarf. "You too Miss. You have a good night," he said as I opened the door for him. "Same to you handsome. Be safe out there." He reached out his arms and I gave him a nice hug and got one good sniff of his neck. My eyes rolled back in my head as I thought: damn that cologne smelled good. I snapped out of my trance and pushed away. I cleared my throat and said "Happy New Year Friend!" "Happy New Year Sunshine!" he said with a smile as he walked out the door. I quickly closed the door behind him and leaned on the back of it. If I stood there any longer with him, New Year's would have been brought in a lot differently.

I get to Raquel's apartment and her old friend from college was there (she was in town to bring in her New Year in the Big Apple.) As I got comfortable, Raquel poured me a glass of wine and asked which dating site I wanted to try next. I hadn't really thought about it much after almost choking to death during my date with AppleBee's King. For me, online dating was like working out at the gym every day, but still eating burgers. Sounds good in theory, but I couldn't really commit. I was straddling the fence until Raquel's friend chimed in. She had met her ex-boyfriend online, but he dumped her after finding a boyfriend of his own on the same site! It wasn't until she told me how therapy was helping her move on, that I decided to get off the fence. I almost died on my first online date; if therapy was going to be next, I say no thank you.

I didn't know what kind of reaction to give to this story, so I opted to run into the bathroom, laugh my ass off silently, and text Robyn that I would be home soon. I could already tell that despite my best efforts, this New Years was a fail, and on top of that, online dating was not looking so good either.

When I came out the bathroom, Raquel was on her phone texting with wide eyes and a huge grin. This guy she had been seeing for a few weeks (another online prospect) told her he wanted to kiss her at midnight when the ball dropped. I have to admit that seeing her run around excitedly, trying to glam herself up, was a little inspiring. If she could get that kind of feeling from a guy she met online, maybe I could too.

Raquel floated off to meet her new potential beau and left me behind with her friend. It was about 11:30 so I decided to stick it out and bring in the New Year warm and safe. As soon as the ball dropped, I hightailed it out of there.

I got home rather quickly as there was no traffic, and arrived in front of my building as Robyn pulled up. She had great timing. "How was Raquel's?" Robyn asked. "Eh, it was an experience. Glad I went. How was church?" I asked. "Eh, it was

an experience. Glad I went," she says, and we both start laughing.
I hadn't gone food shopping and Robyn was trying out a
vegetarian lifestyle, so I threw some crescent roles in the oven
while Robyn cut up some Cracker Barrel sharp cheddar cheese
she found in the fridge. We popped some champagne and danced
to the bands performing on *Dick Clark's New Year's Rockin' Eve*
eating our little cheese sandwiches. We had a blast. Then we
crashed on the couch after a few episodes of *The Honeymooners*. If
this New Year's Eve was any indication of how my year would
go, then I'm all for it. I'm all about enjoying great company,
appreciating what I have, laughing, and living in the moment.

It was a few months into the New Year and I was feeling
great. I was focused on work and going to the gym. I wasn't
losing much weight, but I did lose inches around the midsection
and my clothes fit a lot nicer. Since I was feeling pretty good
about my health and career, I decided maybe it was time I got my
love life in order. I finally got the courage to head back online. I
was going back on Plenty of Fish because, well let's face it, I let
one bad apple spoil the bunch. I also filled out a profile on Ok
Cupid. The Cupid site seemed more polished, which could either
mean the pickings were better or the crazy was hidden better.
Either way there seemed to be more gentlemen on this site. Let
the swiping begin.

The first guy to message me was a 30-year-old French
chef. His profile stated he traveled the world and worked in many
fine dining establishments. His mom was a single parent and

moved him and his 4 sisters to Brooklyn when he was about 13-years-old. He informed me that because he was raised by women he knew how to treat a lady. He had been helping his mother out in the kitchen since he was a toddler and loved it so much he knew from then on that he wanted to be an amazing cook. Since I am greedy and always hungry, I could definitely appreciate a gentleman suitor with skills in the kitchen. He also had a great name. Chef OnALedge. It sounded so French and so chic. I immediately envisioned a life traveling the world with him, eating amazing cuisine and drinking copious amounts of Château Haut-Brion.

Chef and I texted each other all day long. His English was a little shaky, but he was a Frenchman so I was lenient. We agreed that when I got home from work we should FaceTime. His profile picture was of him standing with his arms out in front of the Eiffel Tower so I couldn't really get a good look at his face. I was curious to speak face-to-face with this Black Frenchman. All I knew for sure was if he answered the call wearing a black and white striped v-neck tee shirt with a red scarf tied around his neck, the call would be disconnected promptly.

I told Chef OnALedge I would be home by 6pm and at 6:05 my FaceTime alert went off. I took and deep breath and answered the call. "Wow Shaunie wow! You are so beautiful wow. I can't wait for us to marry and make beautiful children. I will bring you breakfast in bed," Chef OnALedge says, smiling from ear-to-ear. "Hello Chef. You just jump right to it don't you?" I say, giving a fake smile. He didn't look like anything I envisioned and his accent wasn't sexy at all. I let him ramble for a while about spoiling me and how I was the girl of his dreams before I had to interrupt abruptly. "You were born in France? You have an island look about you. Did you grow up in Paris, Nice or Bordeaux? I'm confused," I say pleasantly sarcastic. "No I was born in Haiti and moved to Brooklyn when I was 13. What's your favorite dessert?" he asked, changing the subject. "Red velvet cake, so you're Haitian? Have you ever been to France?" I ask. "No not yet, but I want to go there one day and cook," he says. "So where did you take a picture in front the Eiffel Tower?" I asked beginning to get annoyed. "Las Vegas. I stayed at the Paris. Have you ever been?" he says smiling. I could not stop laughing at myself for being so gullible. I picked up on that Creole immediately, but still wanted to give him the benefit of the doubt. It was at that moment I decided I needed to share this experience with my friends. I was convinced no one would believe me. Since I was talking to him using my iPad, I used my iPhone to record this ridiculous FaceTime call. I needed proof of this load of bologna. I swear as I hit record it was almost like he knew he needed to deliver a performance. He starts licking his lips and says:

"Thank you for giving me the opportunity to get to know you. And I know it takes a lot for you to have even you know step out on that limb. I'm telling you now. I'm on that ledge. I'm standing on that ledge." "Oh boy, be careful," I say being an ass. "Mmm Hmm Oh boy ain't the word. Well you know what. I'm going to leave it up to you. You tell me what's up. What's up?"

Chef says biting his lip and heavily nodding his head. "Okay!" I say. "I want you to tell me Chef OnALedge don't jump," he says laughing. I was hysterical. I could not stop laughing. I had enough footage for my friends to laugh at for a very long time. I ended the call and blocked the Chef. I could only imagine how many women he gave that crazy speech to. I sent the video to my girl Jada and she called me right away because she could not stop laughing. "Sis, where was he FaceTiming you? It looked like he was in somebody's basement." "I don't know, but the connection was spotty. He could be a refugee for all I know trying to get a green card. I can't help him," I say laughing. "Sis I'm keeping this video. It will be my pick me up when I need a laugh between exams," Jada says still cracking up.

I was determined not to give up. My first 24 hours back online I went from fantasizing about traveling the world with a French Chef to FaceTiming with a Haitian refugee in a basement. It could only go up from here.

As I continued to swipe left on the app I was beginning to give up hope until boom Dr4TheKids popped up on my screen. He had a nice smile so I decided to skim his profile. 6'3", college degree yes, career in Pediatrics, lives in Brooklyn, drives but no vehicle, hmm, loves family, and likes to read. This is all pretty good stuff Dr4TheKids. Right swipe for you mister. As soon as I swiped right Cupid pops up, shoots an arrow and puts a heart around our profile pictures. This is so over the top. It was cheesy, but cute at the same time. Apparently he swiped right for me as well so that made us a match. I was scared to send a message so I just continued viewing profiles. A few minutes later

I received a message. It was not from him. It was from LetsPlayPapi. Why did that name sound so familiar? I opened the message and it reads: "Hey gorgeous. I see you're on this site as well. I remember your fine ass from POF. I'm still down to be your boy toy. If you strike out on here too just let me know. I'll be your back-up plan. Take care sexy." What the hell? Back-up plan? And what the hell do you mean strike out on here too? That little overly confident baby gigolo had some nerve. I couldn't reply even after I read the message twice. I was not about to acknowledge his foolery. I decided to just block him. I continued to browse and just as my fingers got tired of swiping left a message appeared from Dr4TheKids.

Hallelujah what the hell took him so long? The message read: "Hello beautiful. My name is Dr.NoNotReally. I enjoyed reading your profile and I'd like the opportunity to set up a date with you." Okay that was simple and to the point. Good job Doc. We chatted every day leading up to the date. He was such a gentleman and his grammar was delightful. He spelled words correctly, used proper punctuation, and he had a nice speaking voice. I was really looking forward to the date. I prayed he looked like his profile picture. I should have FaceTimed or Skyped beforehand. Maybe that would have eased my nerves a little. I decided to wear a classy hot pink knit dress. It covered everything slightly above the knee and hugged every curve, leaving plenty to the imagination. I wore my hair straight because I figured it would complement the sleek look and the weather was on my side because the humidity was low. We were having an early dinner so he made reservations for 6pm. We were dining at Sagaponack which was near my job so there was no excuse for lateness on my part. I suggested we meet in front of the restaurant. This way if we didn't like what we saw, there would be no hard feelings and we could escape easily.

I arrived first at 5:50pm to be exact. I stood near the restaurant, but not directly in front. I figured the getaway would be a lot smoother that way. All of sudden this very tall, slender man who is waiting to cross the street is smiling at me. I gave a nervous smile back. This must be him. Who would just randomly stare at a stranger across the street and smile that hard? I wasn't sure I liked his look yet. He was a lot slimmer than his picture. His smile was nice, but his teeth seemed a little bigger, almost horse like. If I could spot that from across the street imagine up close. He looks better in his picture. While he's crossing the street I could probably just make a run for it. He doesn't look 6'3. Why is this happening? "Hello beautiful. You look just like your picture wow," Dr.NoNotReally says still smiling. "You don't," I say smiling and clenching my teeth. "I'm sorry I didn't hear you," Dr.NoNotReally says as he leans in waiting for me to repeat myself. "I said you don't say. That's one of my fears that someone would say I look better in my picture. That would be so rude to say right? Ha no one wants to hear that. Um let's go in," I say nervously standing, waiting for him to open the door.

We go inside and the restaurant is pretty empty. It was only 6:00pm which is very early for a dinner date. "Hello, hello, hello welcome to Sagaponack. Do you have a reservation?" the maître d asked. "Yes, it should be under the name Dr.NoNotReally. We're a little early." "Hmm don't seem to have a reservation under that name. Hold on, still checking, yeah no. How did you reserve the table?" the maître d asked. At this point my eyes balls were wide open. I knew he was a little embarrassed so I just stepped to the side. I watched as he leaned in to talk to the guy. He wasn't bad looking, it's just I was expecting a more brawny type of man. More Idris Elba-build, less Snoop Dogg. "It appears the lady I spoke to earlier had to leave due to an emergency and didn't write down the reservation in the book. It's all good though, the maître d is going to take care of us," Dr.NoNotReally says with a big smile. "Okay great, oh looks like he's ready for us," I say ready to get this show on the road.

We sit down and I immediately start asking questions about his career. I wanted to know why he chose pediatrics. I love kids so to me that was quite impressive. "So tell me about your work. I think it's great you chose to work with children. My sis Jada is pre-med. Sometimes we don't hear from her for a couple of months because her studying is so intense. It will all be worth it though. I'm so proud of her. Saving a munchkin's life has to be rewarding," I say as I lean forward smiling. Before he could answer the waiter brings our menus. As I stare at the menu I notice it is full of seafood. When I walked in I sensed a beachfront theme, but I just ignored it. "Hmm, this is a seafood restaurant huh?" I say. "Yeah it is. It got 4 stars on Yelp. Uh oh you don't like seafood?" he asked looking concerned. "I'm allergic to shellfish, but that's okay. I see they have short ribs, oh and truffle mash potatoes. Whenever you see truffle you have to eat it. I'm good let's do this," I say confident I wouldn't have to eat again when I got home. "So if I order shrimp is that going to bother you?" he asked. "No the smell doesn't bother me. I just can't eat it. Go on order whatever you want," I say, confirming to myself there would be no kiss at the end of the evening.

We ordered our food and he says, "So you asked me about my job. I love what I do. Finding new ways to teach the kids the importance of eating their fruits and vegetables is very exciting. I want them to think healthy so they will make smarter choices. They enjoy the tours around the hospital." "Tours? How do you have time to give tours? Aren't you busy with appointments and surgeries? Do you sometimes sleep there at the hospital like in *Greys Anatomy?*" I tease, interrupting his interview speech. "No I work 9-5," he says laughing. "Wow you have it really sweet at that hospital. I don't know any doctors with a 9-5 schedule," I say "Oh I'm not a doctor. I want to go back to school and get my PhD in Nutrition and Dietetics. I'm working as a nutrition coach in the pediatrics department of the hospital. I'm looking to move back to South Carolina. That's where my family is originally from. I love NYC, don't get me wrong, but you can have so much more down south. Have you been to South Carolina before?" he asked.

I sipped my cocktail for a while as he rambled about apples, kids, and land in the south. He was very smart, but his profile was a tad misleading. Maybe all I saw was a nice smile, PhD, and pediatrics. Seemed like a good combination at the time.

Now I'm sitting in front of this seafood-loving nutrition coach who wants to move away from the city I love the most. Is that a plastic tie clip? "Have you?" he asks again. I didn't realize I never replied. "You're not a doctor?" I ask. "What? No, but I was asking about South Carolina," he says giving me a side eye squint. "No sorry I've never been to South Carolina. I've never had a desire to visit either. When are you moving?" I ask. At this point, I really just wanted to run in the bathroom and check his profile again. Unfortunately for this site every time you view someone's profile they are notified. There goes being a discrete fact-checker. I still thought he was very nice, but I was losing interest. A nutritionist was a great profession, wait he's a coach, is that the same thing? You know what, forget it. He had a really nice personality and I could hear myself sounding like an asshole. We went on to enjoy the delicious meal and then he challenged me to a game of ping pong after dinner. This nutrition guy was picking up some major points. Slate is a bar lounge located just a few blocks away from the restaurant. They have pool, air hockey, and ping pong. I had stilettos on, but I was certainly up for the challenge.

We get to Slate and the wait was kind of long so we sat in the lounge area. He offered to buy me another drink but I had had two at the restaurant so I reached my online dating drink maximum. We cuddled on the couch and I had a chance to get a really good sniff of his cologne. He smelled good. The more we chatted the more comfortable I felt. "This is taking a long time.

Did you flirt with the girl?" I ask. "Did I what?" Dr.NoNotReally asked laughing. "You heard me. Go over there and get your flirt on. I'm enjoying our conversation don't get me wrong, but I'm ready to kick your butt in ping pong. Now go compliment those funky looking club kid shoes she's wearing and get us a ping pong table," I say seriously. He could not stop laughing. He finally pulls himself together and walks over. I see the girl smile and look down at her shoes. I was hysterical. He takes direction well. Next thing I know he's got two paddles and some balls in his hand and waves me over. "Good job killer! Did you get her number?" I ask. "You are so funny," he says. "Ha, ha hell," I say giving him the side eye.

We put our stuff down and start playing. I was a little rusty so I needed to warm up. Now keep in mind I had 4 inch heels on. He won the first round, but I was the champ in the end. I'm very competitive and talk a lot of mess. I have to make sure I back it up. People were starting to really crowd the place and so the noise level was unbearable. We decided to call it a night. We get outside and it was raining. I was so happy I had flats in my bag. I really needed to figure out when would be a good time to switch into those. We are standing outside and I put my umbrella up. "So which way do you have to walk? Where is your train?" he asked. "My train is east," I said. "Oh okay well my train is west since I live in Brooklyn. I had a really nice time. I hope we can see each other again," he says. As I look at him all I can think was: I know this freaking nutrition coach is not about to let me walk to my train by myself in the dark. "I had a nice time too. Thank you so much," I say smiling while I grit my teeth. And then it happened. He leaned in for a kiss and I leaned back like the matrix. "What's wrong? I don't get a kiss?" he asked. "Um weren't you planning on getting a kiss once you walked me to my train? It's dark," I say with a slight attitude. "That's really out the way for me and I have to get up early in the morning," he says innocently. It was clear he did not feel it was in his gentlemen duties to walk me to my train. So it was clear to me that this would be the last date. God help him if he doesn't check to make sure I got home okay. "Have a good night Dr.NoNotReally," I say as I walk away. I walked about two blocks and my feet were killing me. I had to walk away strong just in case he looked back. I totally doubt he did since he saw nothing wrong with his lack of etiquette. Thank God there was scaffolding so I was able to stop and switch into my flats. I took this time to check my phone. There were a ton of missed calls and text messages from my friends.

Robyn: *Um are you alive? The last text I got from you was I think he's crossing the street oh no.*

Naomi: *Hey baby cakes. How's your evening going with the Doc?*

Victoria: *Sooooo, is he really a doctor? I can totally research his life. I know people!*

Robyn: *If you don't call me by 10pm. I'm calling swat.*

Naomi: *Okay what's going on? Robyn has swat on speed dial and I have body bags. Text us back.*

I texted the girls informing them that I was on my way home and would fill them in once I got into my apartment. I thought the

177

date was okay even though he didn't really look like his picture, wasn't a doctor, has plans to move down south, oh and did I mention he did not walk me to my train? All I'm saying is his chivalry was really half-assed in my opinion. When I got home, I called Robyn and told her everything. Her advice was to set up the next date with someone else. She wanted me to do it during the day so she wouldn't have to worry so much. To hell with what was convenient for me.

The next day I woke up energized. Today was going to be a great day I could feel it. I checked my phone and there was a text from Dr.NoNotReally.

Dr.NoNotReally: *Good morning beautiful. I hope you made it home safely. I had a great time.*

Are you fucking kidding me! I could have died out in these mean streets. Granted I got home around 10pm, but that's not the point. You wait until the next day to check to make sure I was alive. Okay, so the fact that I had that kind of outburst from a single good morning text showed me how I really felt. Dr.NoNotReally would not be seeing me again. So after multiple attempts to answer his text I finally replied with:

Me: *Good morning. Yes I made it home safely. Thank you so much for checking on me this morning. It was so nice meeting you. Take care!*

Dr.NoNotReally: *Lovely meeting you as well.*

I think you could say he got the hint. I decided to check good old Plenty of Fish. I was beginning to feel like I was getting a handle on these dating sites. I never said hello first as an unspoken rule of mine and if you were good looking and wanted to chat, you would have to say more than hello in order to get a response out of me. There was one particular guy who sparked my interest. He was adorable in his pictures, but I was sensing a little arrogance, so when he sent me the "Hello" text I didn't reply. He called himself Mr. Modest. His name was a total contradiction so I didn't bother.

A few days later he said "Hello" again and I was determined to follow my rule. I re-read his profile and checked his pictures again, but I was still hesitant. He did however meet some of the criteria. He was handsome, had a sense of humor, employed, lived alone, and owned a vehicle. I needed more than "Hello." I'm so stubborn sometimes. The next day I got a message from Mr. Modest and it read. "Hello, how are you?" Whoop there it is. I couldn't take it anymore. "Hello Mr. Modest. I'm doing very well. How are you? My name is Shaunie by the way," I replied. "I'm doing much better now that I got a response." Hmm he's flirty and has some spunk. I like it. He continued: "I was wondering if we could grab lunch. Does tomorrow work for you? My name is Framed by the way." "Tomorrow works great. I'm taking a half day so I'll be ready at 1pm," I reply smiling like a jerk. "Looking forward to it, you pick the restaurant and I'll be there," he said. Little did I know that this would be the start of something very special.

#

Chapter 11: Framed aka Mr. Modest

"So guess what? Okay, okay I'll tell you. I'm going on a lunch date with Framed! I'm so excited!" I say, squealing on the phone to Naomi. "Who, what now? Who the hell is Framed? Wait is this the new online interest Mr. Miracles? I thought we were never doing that again," Naomi says. "It's Mr. Modest first of all and did I say never? I don't think I said never. Anyway he's really cute and he's meeting me at Tonic. What color polish should I put on my toes?" I ask. "What are you going to do if this one doesn't look like his picture? Better yet, what if he's a little person, you know representing the lollipop guild? What then? What are the nail polish choices?" Naomi says laughing hysterically. "He will not represent no damn lollipop guild. You got jokes. Are you done? Huh? Are you done? I'm wearing an olive green jumper and gold sandals. The colors are both by Essie. I'm thinking Coral Reef since its summer or Topless and Barefoot because it's a safe nude." "Well you can't go Topless and Barefoot on a first date. You're a lady. Let me get off this phone. Co-workers are harassing my life. Have fun and be kind to little people. Later baby cakes!" Naomi says. "Toodles noodles," I say as I hang up my phone.

Just as I hang up I receive a text from Framed. He wanted to confirm we would still be meeting at 1pm. Since my nails weren't under the dryer yet and it was 12:30, I decided to push our lunch date back to 2pm. I didn't want to rush. I was determined to have a perfect manicure and pedicure. I always mess up one of my nails somehow as soon as I leave the nail salon. He was very mellow about my time change and agreed to meeting at 2pm. Now that I'm thinking about it, he was a little too mellow. What if he used to work in retail and now he collects unemployment so he can go to lunch anytime he wants, but I have to pay? What if he's not 5'9" and he's really 4'9". Great, that's just what I need. Do I really want to date a little man with a big ego? His screen name is Mr. Modest for Christ sakes. I had to take a deep breath. My negative thoughts were consuming me. I had to stop before I ruined something that hadn't even begun. I decided to man up and put on those sandals that pinch the hell out of my pinky toe. If he's a little person, I'll just switch into my flats. See, with positive thinking I was solving problems before they manifested.

I walked over to the restaurant and decided to wait outside. It was a beautiful, warm, sunny day. Not a cloud in the sky. This was perfect weather to dine on a roof top with a little person. Please God let him be 5'9". I was checking Instagram when Framed texted me he was close. I checked a few work emails while I waited. I wanted to look busy when he walked up on me. I looked up and I saw this really handsome, fairly tanned man looking to cross the street. I think this is him. Height is definitely questionable, but he was taller than me and he had a great smile. OMG his ears stick out like little monkey ears. How adorable ooh I like him. "Hello!" I say to the smiling online stranger. "Well hello. It's nice to meet you," Framed said as he went in for the hug. Wow he smells nice. "Shall we go inside?" I say. "After you." Please God don't let me trip. I'm about to get this model strut going as I walk up the stairs. This jumpsuit was very kind to my curves. I hope he appreciates this obvious effort that I'm trying to make seem as subtle as possible.

The waiter takes us to our seats. He let me choose which side of the table I wanted to sit on. Of course I picked the inside seat. I didn't want to sit in the aisle. It's annoying hanging your bag on a seat and people constantly bumping into it. "So thank you for meeting with me today. I was shocked you said yes," Framed said. "Why would I say no? You seem nice and it's only lunch. Is lunch a big deal these days?" I ask, wondering if I should have played a little harder to get. "It's not a big deal you're right. I like that it was an easy decision for you. Meeting you was an easy decision for me. You're actually the first person I've met from online," Framed said as he looked up at me while he sipped his Coke. Damn he's a cutie. "I am? Really? Wow! Am I the only person you wanted to meet or was I the only person to say yes?" I asked giving him the side eye. He laughed. "A little of both." Okay, sense of humor I see. You are racking up the points little modest man. He says he's 5'9", but I'm thinking more like 5'7". Yes two inches makes a big difference. "How's the steak here?" Framed asked. "Oh I don't know. I've never had it here. I do know the mac and cheese is yummy and so is the spicy chicken wrap," I say smiling. I really wanted that mac and cheese. I was starving. "Well I'm a steak connoisseur. I know all the best steak places in NYC. Would you have a steak with me?" he asked. "I wouldn't eat a whole one on my own, but I would have a piece of yours if that's okay," I say. "Hmm okay we can split one, but you're getting your own mac and cheese. If it's as good as you say it is, I'm not sharing that," Framed said smiling. As he ordered our food he was very comical with the waiter. He had a big personality for sure and I enjoyed it. I liked him already.

As we split our steak, we discussed our careers. Turns out he had just started his new job about 4 months ago. He was the store manager for one of the biggest retail giants in the world. I think the coolest part of listening to him talk about his career was that he absolutely loved what he did for a living and the company he worked for. His eyes lit up when he talked about the growth opportunities with this retail giant. I had vowed to never work retail again, but I have to admit it sounded more appealing coming from someone who wasn't the low man on the totem pole. His ambition oozed out of him and I thought it was extremely sexy.

"What time do you have to get back?" I asked. I didn't want this lunch to end. "I want to be back at 3. I have a meeting and well, I don't want to take advantage," Framed said. "Oh I understand. It's always good to impress your boss," I say. "I am the boss," Framed said. "Well excuse me. Practicing what you preach. Those are signs of a great leader. Nice!" I say, very impressed. "Thank you," he blushed as he continued. "We stayed here longer than I thought we would. Now I have to rush back, but it was worth it." "Well since you have to rush then I'll put on my flats. I'm heading that way as well. My train is on the way." "Copy. So I get to spend more time with you on our really fast walk," Framed said smiling. I giggled. I felt like such a girly girl around him. I haven't felt like that since well, Superman. I changed my shoes and we were off. We talked about meeting for lunch again soon. We got to my train and we hugged. He was a great hugger. We didn't want to leave one another, but I loved that he was forcing himself to be responsible. That man had career goals and I certainly wanted to be supportive. I smiled all the way home.

The next day I was at work chatting with Sasha at reception. It was around 12 o'clock and Framed texted me:

Framed: *Hello. What time do you take lunch today?*

"OMG it's him, it's him," I say to Sasha while I fix my hair. "OMG, it's Mr. Marvelous? I'm so excited for you. Fix your necklace," Sasha says. "It's Mr. Modest, Sasha, Mr. Modest," I say with a blank stare. "Sorry!" Sasha says as she puts her head down. "He wants to know what time I go to lunch." "Tell him whenever you want because you got it like that," Sasha says. "Right, okay," I say nodding my head right before I respond.

Me: *Hey handsome, anytime between 12 and 2.*

Framed: *Okay can I take you to lunch at 1pm?*

Me: *Sure I'd like that.*

Framed: *Copy, I'll come to you.*

Me: *Okay cool*

"So since you were doing all of that smiling while on your phone, I take it you're meeting Modest Man for lunch?" Sasha asks batting her eyes. "You're so sassy and absolutely right. Hell yeah I am! I have to go answer some emails before I head out for my lunch date. Emphasis on the word date!" I say as I shimmy toward the elevators. Sasha could not stop laughing at me. As I walked back to my desk I couldn't get over the fact that this man wanted to see me the next day. I really must have left a good impression. He certainly left one on me.

1pm arrived and we met at California Pizza Kitchen. We were so excited to see each other. Little did we know lunches and quick meet ups after work would be our thing. Our dates were always spontaneous, short, and fun. Each time we saw each other we created another moment, another memory, and saw each other in another light. Our relationship was light and fluffy, smiles and laughter. He was very private, but he opened up to me a little more each time. We were moving slow and that's just what I wanted. After all, I was working two jobs and my event season was getting a bit intense. My life was made of lots of heavy planning, schedule juggling, and traveling. I didn't have time for a serious relationship, and the way he was excelling in his career, neither did he. He was offered a huge promotion after 5 months of working for the retail giant, but he turned it down because he wanted to learn more about the company. He wanted to be the best at what he did and wanted more training. I was so proud of him for making such a smart decision. I would have took the promotion and figured that shit out as I go. I was also happy I was the first person he shared the news with. Framed is a good looking guy, but he has such a beautiful mind. I was so attracted to his way of thinking. He had business know-how and was always thinking of ways to improve himself.

One day I got out of work a little early and we decided we would meet up for happy hour. 33rd street seemed to be our neutral ground. He would head east and I would head north. Every time without fail, I would rush to get to him. I didn't want to be late. As usual I almost walked right past him. "Slow down. Hi I'm right here, I love that you always walk with purpose," he'd say. It was the New Yorker in me. I'm always in a rush. I couldn't help it. There was a cute bar near Tonic where we had our first date. "This place looks cool. Drinks half price. Wanna give it a go?" I asked.

I decided to wear a dress that day. Autumn was in full bloom. It was just cold enough outside to wear Spanx without becoming a sweat ball, so everything was tight and well put together. I was ready to sit and sip pretty. We walked in and he led me to the back. I let him take the inside seat this time since it was a bench, but I gave him my jacket and bag to place next to him. Before I could take my seat he said, "You look nice. I like your dress. Come here. Can I have a hug?" It was such a simple compliment followed by a smooth request, but it made me blush. "Of course you can," I say leaning in for the hug. His embrace was so tight, like he didn't want to let go. I could feel him sniff my hair as he squeezed tighter. "You smell so good. What is that you're wearing?" Framed asked. "It's a secret combo. I never tell," I say trying to be mysterious and flirtatious. "Copy." "Copy, what is that? You always say that," I said. "Do I really? I'm sorry. It's a term we use on the job. Guess the retail lingo is sticking with me. Question for you. Can I have a kiss?" Framed asked. I smiled for a while, surprised at the question. Usually these dudes lean in and just try to take it. Many have tried. Many have failed. I leaned in about 30 %. He had to work for it a little. He came in the other 70% and nailed it. Chills ran down my spine. It wasn't sloppy or wet. I hate when guys try to suck in your whole face. I should not need a face cloth after a kiss. What the hell was wrong with them? That wasn't the case for Framed. Our first kiss was amazing. First he hooked my mind and now he's trying to hook my body. Jesus take the wheel.

The waitress came over and we placed our drink order. Framed asked me to sit next to him on the cushioned bench. I always thought that was so over the top when couples sat on the same side of the table. You certainly wouldn't think so the way I hopped up out my chair. I practically sat on the man's lap. We drank the mediocre drinks and he ordered nachos and chicken tenders. We laughed and shared stories about our younger days. Then I asked, "So how many children do you want? You do like munchkins, right?" I asked, holding my breath waiting for the response. "Um, yeah. Two I guess," he says. "Really that's great. I always felt the ideal situation would be to have twins. One boy, one girl and done. Body snaps back," I say snapping my fingers. "That would be perfect," Framed said, chuckling at my excitement.

It was getting late and we were told by the waitress that there was a group coming in that would occupy the entire back area, including the section we were sitting in. We decided we should probably call it an evening. Framed told me he was going to the bathroom and asked if I wanted to join him. I giggled at the idea. After all people only did that kinky stuff in the movies right? I waited 5 minutes and I followed him downstairs. There were 3 restrooms. Since the sinks were in a communal space, we washed our hands for a while to make sure we were the only ones down there. When the coast was clear, Framed took my hand and pulled me into one of the restrooms. Thank God it was clean and very posh.

He locked the door, pinned me to the wall and kissed me so passionately my toes curled. He started kissing on my neck and grabbing my butt and then his hand starting creeping up my dress. That's when I panicked. Oh shit, oh shit, oh shit! He's going to feel my Spanx! I immediately broke free from his grip and pinned him against the wall instead. Biting his ear and rubbing all over him. I could tell he loved it by the way he kept biting his lip and grabbing a fist full of my hair. I was so turned on from his touch that when he attempted to lift my dress I said "screw it." He would see the body armor one day anyway, plus he wouldn't be able to get to the goodies. These Spanx were a chastity belt tonight. "What is this scuba wear?" he asked panting. "Spanx," I said as I bit his lip. "Copy" he said, and then he lifted me up and I wrapped my legs around his waist. Somehow that little minx got a few fingers up my thigh, past the

Spanx, I had to shut it down. I was not about to let my first time having sex with this man be in a restaurant bathroom. "What's the matter? What happened?" he asked, with his member hanging out. I couldn't help but look at it. I was impressed he got that anaconda out so quickly. "Put that away," I said while fixing my Spanx and pulling down my dress. Once I adjusted the girls and my hair I said, "I'm a lady. Control yourself." We both started laughing. We couldn't believe what came over us. We kissed softly as he pulled his pants up. We kept adjusting each other and then the moment of truth came. Who was going to exit first? We listened at the door and when we thought the coast was clear, Framed exited first. I just leaned on the door waiting for my cue to come out. All I could think was, I'm so deleting my online dating profile. He would be too tough of an act to follow.

"OMG I can't believe you made out in the bathroom. You nasty!" Robyn said giggly over the phone. "I know right! In our defense it was a nice restroom. It's not like we were in some random stall. Besides I really like him. He's so smart. I feel like we have a real connection. I'm enjoying myself!" I say blushing. "It sounds like someone is a smitten kitten. Are you sure you want to delete your profile though? It's only been a couple of months, if that," Robyn asked. "Yeah I'm sure. I want to see what happens. His ambition is so, so, so sexy. I love it!" I say squealing. Robyn could not stop laughing.

About two weeks later, I decided to have lunch with an old acquaintance. We always say we should meet up, but it never happens. Nia was a member at the gym I used to work at years ago. We kept saying we were going to do lunch since we worked in the same neighborhood. Well, 3 years later it finally happened. We were so excited we were actually going to follow through and have girl talk over a meal. Nia and I had just finalized our plans at Vezzo when Framed texted me.

Framed: *Good morning. Are you available for a quick lunch today? I'm in your area.*

Me: *Sure what time?*

Framed: *In the next ten minutes?*

Me: *Okay cool. Where shall we meet?*

Framed: *25th and Madison.*

Me: *Okay I'll start walking down.*

Framed: *Copy.*

Just that fast my lunch plans with Nia slipped my mind. I was determined to keep my word. Can I just say that the stars aligned that day? Just as I finished my thought, Nia texted me, asking if we could push the lunch back to 1pm. I couldn't have planned it better myself. As usual I'm rushing and run smack into Framed. He loved me running into him and to this day I don't understand why. We talked about how our days were going and he told me all about his important meeting. We decided to go to Starbucks to warm up. I already informed him of my lunch plans with Nia. As much as I wanted to be available to him as often as I could, I wouldn't allow myself to do it. He was a busy man and I was a busy lady. We would have to just get in where we fit in.

I found us a table while he ordered our drinks. "One more time, latte what?" Framed asked. "Grande Chai Tea Latte. Come on man get it together," I say teasing. He comes to the table and sets our drinks down. "So what else is new with you?" Framed asked. "There's not much going on. I have a big wine tasting coming up so the office is a little crazy. I have to work my second job tonight. Hopefully my friends are also working tonight so the time will fly by. Let's see, I have lunch at 1pm eh em. Oh and I'm happy to spend some time with you of course. What's new with you? You look like something is on your mind," I say giving him a wide-eyed stare as I sip my tea. After a quick back and forth of me repeating the question and him responding with nothing, he finally says, "You know what I find interesting? You asked me just about every question except for one. You never asked if I have kids." I immediately put my tea down. "Why would I ask you that? Your profile said you didn't. It had to, because I specifically did not answer anyone who answered "yes" or "rather not say" to that question," I said, second-guessing myself. I couldn't go back and check. We'd both deleted our profiles. "Really? I mean you asked me how many I wanted and if I liked them, but you never asked me if I had any," Framed said, looking a little uneasy. "Well do you? Do you have a kid?" I asked gripping my tea with both hands as I braced myself for the response. "I have two," Framed said staring deep into my eyes.

Oh no! How could I have missed that? He totally skipped that question. There is no way I would have replied to his message if he'd said he had two kids.. Okay Shaunie it's not the end of the world. At least find out what they are. Maybe it's two boys and he wants to try for a girl one day. "Hello. Say something please," Framed says, leaning in closer. "Two, wow okay, okay. How old?" I ask praying he doesn't say newborns. "My daughter is 9 and my son is 4," he says. My heart sunk into my stomach. Suddenly I couldn't care less about being on time for my lunch with Nia. I just wanted to lie down. All those butterflies I felt with him were now making me ill. "Same mother?" I asked. "Yes remember I told you my ex and I are like best friends," he said.

He was so soft-spoken, but I couldn't seem to find comfort in his soothing tone. "Well let me see the little munchkins! Do you have pictures?" I asked, trying to find my smile. "Yes of course," he said as he pulled out his phone. I looked at the picture. They were real. You could even see the personalities through the picture. "Wow look at them. Do you want to have more?" I asked. I held my breath hoping his reply would bring my lost smile back. Framed stared at me for a while. Then he shook his head and said, "No. I really don't want anymore." Just like that my future plans with Framed were shattered. There was no romantic future for him and I. I was sad and really wanted to run out of there, but it was so cold and my tea was making me feel so warm and toasty. "Wow, so now what do we do?" I asked. "I don't know. I don't want to hold you back, but I don't want to let you go," he said sincerely. He looked sad. I could tell it was never his intention to hurt me so I said, "Well I guess we'll just have to be friends." His entire body sulked. Clearly that was not what he wanted to hear. "I was afraid you would say that." "Yeah well it's the best I can offer at this time. You've basically told me there is no future with you. I already really like you, so it will be an adjustment. Damn!" I said.

I couldn't hide my disappointment. I couldn't understand why I would have to ask if he had kids. Why wouldn't he just tell me from the beginning? If I sat there any longer I would sulk all day. "I have to go. Lunch plans remember and you sir have to get back to the store. Thank you for the tea. It really warmed me up," I say struggling to button my coat. My hands were shaking. I was having a hard time pulling myself together. We get outside and Framed's coat was wide open. I guess I must have really rushed us out of there. I pulled him close to me and zippered up his jacket. "You already said you feel like you're catching a cold. Don't encourage it," I say. Right as I was about to take off he pulled me close, kissed me on the cheek, and said, "You're awesome, you know that? You're very special to me. Okay?" I smiled and said, "Yeah I know." I winked for dramatic affect and darted across the street. There were cars coming ready to run me over, but I didn't care. I had to get away. I channeled my inner Tina Turner and ran across that street and kept running for about half a block. I was winded. Damn! I need to get back in the gym I thought.

When I caught my breath, I called Naomi. I told her everything that just happened with Framed. She must have heard the devastation in my voice because she went off. "That motherfucker! How could he not tell you that in the beginning? What was he thinking? That is pertinent information. You shouldn't have to ask shit like that. He should have told you that on date 1,2,3,4 not on date 35 or however many you two are on. Do you count every "meet and greet" as dates? Doesn't matter, the point is he lied. You were an open book and he just let you tell all your business and not share his. That's some selfish shit. Something in my soul would not let me get all giddy about this dude for you. Ugh I'm so pissed." Here I am calling Naomi for comfort and I ended up comforting her. "I know, but I really like him. It's disappointing there won't be a romantic future, but I don't think he's a bad person. I told him we could still be friends," I say, feeling completely drained. "He doesn't deserve you as a friend Shaunie. You're too nice," Naomi says with an attitude. "I know, I know, but I have to get off the phone. I'm meeting my friend Nia for lunch. I'll hit you up later," I say as I walk up to the restaurant. "Who the hell is Nia? You're always making new friends. What am I going to do with you? Enjoy your lunch baby cakes," Naomi says as she hangs up the phone.

Nia and I enter the restaurant and decide to have a glass of white wine with our quinoa salad. We laughed and talked about everything under the sun. We even discussed my recent news from Framed. "Wow! Well from what you're telling me, it sounds like you still really like him. He might have been afraid to tell you since you are so open and the ideal woman for him. Listen I've been with my man for 8 years, and he has 6 kids by 4 different women. We don't have any together, but he knows I would want to have some one day and he's open to it. I love him and we have a happy life together. Everyone is respectful for the most part. Right now I'm enjoying my freedom, just as you should. Shit at least it's only 2 kids," Nia says as she sips her wine. It made me wonder if I was overreacting. I mean, at this age if I really wanted to have kids, wouldn't I have done it already? Let's be real here. There really isn't a perfect time to have a child. I guess my disappointment isn't that he had kids already. One girl and one boy, might I reiterate, but it's the fact that he's against having another one. I'm not being greedy. I'd be happy with one with my eyeballs and his ears. That would be the cutest munchkin ever. Get a grip Shaunie. "Damn it man!" I say out loud and chug my wine.

It took a little while for me to get over the news, but Framed and I kept talking. We actually developed a real friendship. We would make out every now and then, but we agreed sex was off the table. Why should we practice baby making if he didn't want to have any more babies. Plus I knew it would be good. There was so much passion between us, how could it not. Our outings became very sporadic. Both of our jobs were becoming more demanding, so we would go weeks without seeing each other.

One day, Framed texted me, asking where I was. He wanted to see me. I told him that I decided I needed a new dress to wear to this black tie wine banquet for my job. Perhaps he could help me make a final decision. I found the dress I had been stalking online. It was at Nordstrom Rack. It was the only one left and it was my size. Some things are just meant to be. I bought the dress immediately. When Framed arrived, I was done.

195

"You bought it already?" Framed asked. "Yep! Sorry Charlie!" I say patting the bag. "So you're not going to let me see you try it on? No modeling in your underwear, nothing? Open the bag let me see?" he says, peeking in the bag. I laughed and opened the bag. "I'm not pulling this whole thing out. I'll show you the picture on my phone," I say as I pull out my phone. I showed him the picture and he told me I was going to look beautiful in it. He always gave such simple compliments, but they meant more to me coming from him. "Let's go get a cupcake or something. I feel like I should treat you to something sweet. Want to?" he asked. I loved his randomness. "Sure. I can't say no to baked goods." As usual we started walking in a random direction and fell into this charming bakery. I shared my tiramisu and he shared his lemon tart. We both had a cappuccino. I asked him to create something in the foam. He tried to make a design. It wasn't very good, but I enjoyed watching him try.

Another time we met, it was a frigid night in the city. I enjoy taking random walks in Manhattan after work, just to take in the scenery. Framed and I met on 34th street. He had had a bit of a rough day and wanted to do a little shopping. We went in and out of stores. Unfortunately we missed all the sample sales; they closed early. We ended up in Banana Republic. We walked in and he spotted a really cool quilted vest. He examined it, but ended up leaving it on the rack. He found a navy blue cardigan with leather paneling that caught his eye. The man had taste. He asked me to go into the dressing room with him while he tried it on. Of course we made out in the dressing room. We kept it as PG as possible, but it was definitely steamy. Before he purchased the sweater he looked for the vest again. It was gone. He seemed a little disappointed standing on line waiting to make his purchase. I asked a sales person if they were getting anymore in. He said no, it was a popular item, and was sold out. I made it my mission to find that vest. I don't take no for an answer.

As we walked a few blocks chatting away I spotted a cupcake bakery. My eyes must have lit up and he noticed. "You want a cupcake?" Framed asked. I nodded yes and smiled like a big kid. We each got a cupcake and ate it on the bench outside the bakery. I was starting to think he was creating these moments on purpose.

About two weeks later, I met him for a Sunday Lunch. We hadn't seen each other in a while and I had a meeting in the city with Job2 so seeing him would be easy. We ended up having lunch at a diner near his store. "Somebody did a little shopping I see," he says looking at my bag. "Oh yes I did. Wanna see what I got?" I asked, trying to contain my excitement. "Sure let me see." I passed Framed the bag and this big smile appeared on his face. "You are very sweet, you know that? Thank you. I can't believe you found the vest. Wow!" "You're welcome. I wanted you to have it. It's just a little something for always treating me and being a gentleman," I say beaming. Nothing beats giving. After lunch he walked me to my car and yes, we made out. I felt like such a school girl with him. After all, it's just innocent fun with a great guy. What's the harm in that?

\#

Chapter 12: Happy Birthday Framed

"You're playing with fire. Please be careful. You know you wear your heart on your sleeve Shaunie," Naomi says over the phone. "I am being careful. Framed is a cool guy. I told you he came out to the city the other night with his friend? I was out with Miranda and a few other girls from Job2 and he showed up," I say smiling. "And how did he know where you were miss missy?" Naomi asked. "Huh? He texted me, he asked what I was doing and I told him," I say innocently. "Oh I see, like the time we went out for the boozy brunch and your tipsy ass wanted McDonald's fries afterward. Robyn and I go order the food and we come back to find Mr. Miracles sitting at the table with you. You mean like that?" Naomi says quite sassy. "Exactly! I can't help it if Mr. MODEST was in the area." "Oh I bet you can't. You're not slick," Naomi says laughing. "Listen here okay. We are friends. I'm seeing other people." "Oh yeah. Who?" Naomi asked. "Um..." I say thinking really hard. "You see? You're being faithful to someone you're not even in a relationship with. Don't put all your eggs in his basket. They won't get fertilized baby cakes." "Low blow Peppermint Petty. You're right though. I know you're right. I just feel like a moth to a flame. Ugh so frustrating. I'm going to get my life together," I say. "You better with your flaming ass. I have to get back to work Hun. I'll check on you later," Naomi says as she hangs up the phone.

Naomi was absolutely right. What the hell was I thinking?

I wasn't trying to meet anyone new. I was content with seeing him when it was convenient for him. This can't be right. My event season had died down and I had a little more time on my hands. I started to notice things that I guess I ignored early on because I was so busy. Like the fact that we have never gone on a real evening date. You know, the "pick you up, I made reservations, you look amazing, would you like sparkling or still water" kind of date. Granted we were friends now, but the few months before the munchkin news, we still hadn't had a real date. He never called me in the evening and I'd never been to his place. Oh sweet baby Jesus. Is he married? Nooo, no freaking way. I mean I know he said he was engaged before but no, he wouldn't lie to me. The "don't ask don't tell" policy only works in the army. Not out here in these dating streets.

The next day Framed and I decided to meet up for one of our impromptu Starbucks jaunts. I was excited to see him. We were in the friend zone, so asking if he was married wouldn't be a big deal right?

"Hello. You look nice. I like your hat," Framed says going in for the hug. "Hi. Are you married?" I asked. It was like I had tourettes. I had to let it out immediately. "No! Nice to see you too, where did that come from? Let's go inside it's cold out here," he says opening the door. "You're sure?" I ask, not breaking eye contact. "Yes I'm sure. What's going on?" he asked with a confused look. "Nothing, I just started noticing some things and all signs point to married man. No late night calls, no random trips to the movies, no apartment visits, and what the hell happened to my special steak dinner you promised me?" I say with an attitude. "Okay you know I work a lot. I go to bed early. Honestly I hardly ever go to the movies because I don't have time. I don't invite women to my home. Although for you I am really considering breaking that rule. I just don't want to put us in a compromising situation. As for the steak dinner I apologize. I do owe you that. The job has just been so demanding. I promise I will take you. I want it to be special. Any more questions detective?" Framed asks with a half-smile. "No we're good. Thanks for explaining," I say, still feeling a little uneasy. We decided to get hot apple cider and head downstairs so we can sit and talk some more. "Question for you. If you thought I was married, why did you continue to speak with me for so long?" Framed asked. Oh he's good. "Oh you're good. Honestly I didn't want to believe it. I really like you and I wanted to give you the benefit of the doubt. Then my thoughts started to get the best of me even though we're just friends. I figured I'd ask to alleviate any confusion.". "Copy, well I'm not. I'm glad we've cleared that up. So tell me what's new?" Frame says as he begins to doodle on a napkin.

While we're laughing and chatting, this huge 6'4" 300 lb. guy is going to each table asking people for money. He looked really mean. I guess he was trying to look intimidating. It seemed to be working for the other tables. He was certainly collecting. Then I guess it was our turn. Framed and I continued talking. While I'm teasing him about his doodle, the guy asks "You have twenty dollars?" Framed and I looked at each other with wide eyes then turned to him and said. "No sorry." We went back to talking and he was still standing there. He looked us up and down, leans in a little and says, "You don't have twenty dollars?" I was taken aback by his boldness. Why would he ask us twice? I'm sure he wasn't asking the other tables for twenty dollars. I was pissed. "No WE don't." Framed said very stern and dismissive. We looked at each other with the wide eye stare again and tried to continue our conversation yet again. The guy looked mad, but he walked away and continued to beg more tables. "Twenty dollars?" Framed and I said at the same time and burst into laughter. "That took balls. I know he didn't ask the other tables for twenty dollars. Did he think we were going to be scared?" I asked. "I don't know what he thought, but it was not going down today. Like I was going to say, here sir, just take my whole wallet. Get the fuck outta here," Framed said laughing. "So let me see this picture you've drawn," I say as Framed slides over the napkin. "A candle? Wow you even drew the holder and the wax is dripping. What is that flying? You're pretty talented sir. What does this represent?" "Moth to a flame," Frame says innocently, smiling at me. Oh shit!

Winter was amongst us. Snow was everywhere and the city looked so beautiful. The office had moved and we were now located on the west side of Manhattan. It added another 20 minutes to my commute, but it wasn't bad. On the east side, our office was in a quiet neighborhood. My co-workers and I would often complain about it being boring and not having any convenient places to shop. We would either have to head to Union Square or walk all the way to 34th street for some retail action. It is so true that you don't miss a good thing until it's gone. Now we were in the middle of tourist land. Time Square was a few blocks south. Rockefeller Center was a few blocks east and Columbus Circle was a few blocks north. We are now in the center of it all. Random meet-ups with Framed were definitely few and far between. We became a little more distant during the holiday season. I know in retail the holidays are everything, so I didn't pay it too much attention. I stopped myself from asking if he wanted to grab a quick bite or Starbucks. It would either slip his mind that we had plans or he canceled saying he just couldn't get out of the office. He'd just taken a promotion so his responsibility had tripled. One thing I firmly believe in is you always make time for things you really want to do. So after hearing "I can't" so many times, I stopped asking to meet. This girl can take a hint.

It was a brisk Friday morning and I received a random text from Framed. I was taken aback by it since he had been so distant. My reply was not very warm and inviting. I was pretty much over his inconsistency.

Framed: *Good morning. How are you?*

Me: *Good morning. I'm fine.*

Framed: *I'm off today. Finally, what's on your agenda today?*

Me: *Nice. I hope you enjoy. I'm heading into work.*

Framed: *Can you play hooky today?*

Me: *Nope I have meetings scheduled. The wine tour and cigar dinner is in a few months. No days off.*

Framed: *Oh okay I understand.*

Me: *Have a great day.*

Framed: *You too.*

The nerve of him! He hadn't reached out to me for weeks. Now he expects me to just take a day off. I loved the spontaneity of it, but I wouldn't allow myself to give in. Had he been consistent, I would, at the very least, have taken a half day, but I had responsibilities too. As much as I would have loved to spend the day with him I couldn't.

I got to work and was glad I went. The meetings cleared some things up with the upcoming events and I really felt like I was on top of it all. The day miraculously flew by. I planned to go to the gym when I got home. I really wanted to stick with my workout regimen.

While climbing the stair master, I just kept thinking about Framed's request. I couldn't believe I was still in shock. Part of me felt like I should have taken advantage of the opportunity, but then again, I couldn't help but wonder if he would have taken a day off for me. The sad part is I knew the answer and would never pose the suggestion. I decided to put in extra work at the gym. I had brunch with Naomi on Sunday and I was not holding back. Unlimited sangria and empanadas! I was going to enjoy myself.

"We'll have red this time!" Naomi says to the bartender before she continues. "I told his ass 'look we are not about to be one of those boring couples.' So we are going to Trinidad for his birthday and I am packing strings and things. He better get on board with it because I'm celebrating with or without him," she said as she sipped her red sangria. "You go girl! That'll teach him. What's the lesson here again?" I ask giggling. "I can't stand you. The lesson is I'm fun and still young and we need a change of scenery and I've never been to Trinidad and I really, really, really want to go," she said, slamming down her glass.

"You know what I just thought about? I met StickyFingers here," I say looking around. "Ugh I know. I'm trying to forget that. What's up with Superman? I haven't heard anything about him lately." Naomi asks, giving me the side eye. "We are really being platonic. I haven't seen him in months. That's a good thing though. He's out being the perfect family man," I say slamming down my glass. "Easy killer. Speaking of family man, what's up with Little Bit of Luck?" Naomi asks. We both start laughing. Even the bartender giggled at that one. "Who wants white sangriaaaaaa?" the bartender yells and of course Naomi and I are the first to raise our glasses. "He texted me last Friday. He wanted to know if I wanted to play hooky. I declined. I hadn't heard from him in weeks. I thought the request was pretty ballsy don't you?" I say. "He's got some nerve. I'm proud of you for not going. I know you probably would have jumped at the chance if he played his cards right." "Yeah I would have. I think his birthday is coming up. I'm not sure when. You know how you ask people when's your birthday? And they say shit, like oh in two weeks. Like really? I'm not asking for a count down. I'm asking for your actual date of birth. Anyway it's close, but I'm not sure when. I should rename him Captain Vague," I said, as I roll my eyes. "Go ahead. I rename Tiny Tim all the time. So are you going to ask him when his birthday is?" Naomi asked. "He's 5'9", 5'7" whatever. No I'm not going to ask again. I feel like I've asked twice and both times he neglected to share, so I'll just randomly text him happy birthday and see what happens," I say shrugging my shoulders. "You're an ass. I swear I can't stand you. Let's get out of here. I want a donut," Naomi says laughing.

I always enjoy brunch with my friends. We have so much fun and the bartenders love us. By the time we are ready to leave, we never know our ass from our elbows, but we do know we had a great time.

Later in the week I texted Framed happy birthday and he thanked me. Hmm nailed it! I asked if he was free Sunday and if he wanted to have lunch. He said he had to work, but agreed anyway, proving the theory you always make time for the things you want to do. I take it he missed me because he was making an effort despite his crazy schedule.

That Sunday the weather was bad. There was a wintry mix, with slush and ice everywhere. These conditions are the absolute worst when your car doesn't have all-wheel drive. I took a chance driving into the city anyway. I refused to take the subway on the weekends. Trains run slower and that's if they are running at all. Framed and I decided to meet on 9th Avenue. I knew I wouldn't be able to find parking on 7th. He got in the car and there was a parking space in front of a cute diner. We decided it would be best to park and eat there. I am a strong

205

believer in signs. That space was meant for me. I did too much slipping and sliding to get there. It was God's way of telling me to go sit down somewhere and be still.

We grab a booth and decide to have breakfast for lunch. I had pancakes with tea and he had bacon and an omelet. "So did you enjoy your birthday?" I ask sipping my tea. "It was okay. I was trying to spend it with you, but you gave me the cold shoulder," he says examining his fork. "Pardon? When was your birthday? I don't recall an invite," I say slightly offended. "Last Friday. Remember I texted you to see if you wanted to play hooky. You were mean. Ring a bell?" he says, switching his utensil set with the one on the next table. "Oh my goodness, are you serious? I feel so bad. Seriously?" "Yep. You want me to help clean the egg off your face? It's okay. You're kind of a jerk," Framed says laughing. "I am so sorry. In my defense you never gave me your actual birth date anyway," I say with my nose in the air. "I'm pretty sure I did. It's cool, just another day. I finally had the day off and I wanted to spend it with you, but no worries. I'll be fine," he said, putting his head down. "Oh you are laying it on thick mister. So dramatic!" I say as I checked my phone. I had a text from my mom. She had sent me and my brothers a picture of my grandfather posing with some lounge singer. "Ha, this man does not stay still. I swear I want to be like him when I grow up." "Who are you talking about?" Framed asked. "My grandpa!" I say as I pass him the phone. Framed starts laughing and says, "Nice. He looks so young." "Black don't crack. Look at me. I don't look a day over newborn," I say cracking myself up. Framed kept my phone and his fingers kept typing away. When I tried to reach for it he would pull away. When he finally gave it back, it was a meme of my grandfather with the caption: Pimping ain't easy. I could not stop laughing. I sent it to my mom and brothers.

Framed asked to see my phone again. I gave it to him, figuring he would make another meme. This time he was taking a little longer. He better not go through my messages. I don't have anything to hide, but still. I began to get nervous anyway. I felt so exposed. "Here," Framed says, passing me my phone. "What did you do?" I say giving him the evil eye. "Go ahead and type my name like you're sending me a message," he says smiling. "What?" I asked confused. "Just try it." I begin to type his name and this entire message popped up. It read: Even though I'm a jerk for forgetting his birthday it's okay because he really likes me anyway. "Are you kidding me with this?" I ask laughing. "Nope. Every single time you begin to type my name that message will appear in the text and you'll have to delete the whole message so you can say what you really want to say. Bet you won't forget my birthday next year," Framed says laughing. "You're horrible for this. I don't even know how to take this off. What are you looking at?" I say, quite sassy. "Was I staring? I like your face." I just blushed and continued to eat my pancakes.

Our time was up and he had to get back to work. We get outside and the flurries were still coming down. He gives me a big hug and tells me how pretty I look. "You should let me take your picture. Stand still," Framed says. "Oh no, no, no I'm sure my hair looks crazy now. I'll take one if you take it with me."

"Oh no, I don't like taking pictures. They never come out right," Framed says and we start walking to the car. I drove him to work slowly. My car slid a little even though I was driving like a little old lady. The slushy conditions were ridiculous. When he was getting out the car he kissed me good bye and bumped his head on my sunroof trying to get out quickly. I pretended I didn't notice. He dashed across the street and I waited to make sure he didn't bust his butt running in this messy weather. I proceeded to drive off when he texted me that he had a great time and was happy to see me. I smiled all the way home.

Since I still had an uneasy feeling about his relationship status, I decided maybe I should do a little digging. We had known each other for a little over 6 months now and we had no pictures together. That may not sound like a big deal to most, but to a snap happy Sally like me, it was major. Friends take pictures together all the time. Something was up. He told me he didn't use social media really. He only had a LinkedIn account and a Facebook account that he never used. I have Facebook and I never use mine either. So that much I believed. One thing I learned from BagelBoy was that men with something to hide will lie for as long as possible to keep you in the dark. The saying goes "what you do in the dark will come out in the light." Well, let there be light.

"Hey doll, I need to know if Framed is married, still engaged, in a relationship whatever. Is he taken? Tell Sissy I said go, go, gadget," I say to Naomi laughing. "It's about damn time. You know my sister lives for shit like this. We're on it. Let the investigation of Messy Miracles begin," Naomi says laughing.

"You're an ass. I love it though. Let me know the minute you make a discovery." "One question for you, Hun. Why now?" Naomi asks. "Because I really like him and my gut won't let me relax. If he's lying, I'd rather know now. This will let me know if our friendship is real." "Okay baby cakes. I hope we don't find anything," Naomi says. "Yeah, you and me both," I say as I hang up the phone.

About 4 days later, I'm at work and needed to check our bag inventory. My co-worker Liza accompanied me to our storage room to see if we had any messenger bags for this seminar we were conducting. On our way downstairs, I tell Liza about the current investigation on Framed. "I hate to say this to you, but it sounds like he's married or at the very least lives with the girl. Remember I asked you if he was married months ago," Liza says. "I want to believe him, but I'm having trouble. Maybe if he wasn't so vague I wouldn't feel this way. I mean, I'm cool right? I handled the kid bomb pretty well," I say, trying to convince myself. "Yeah you did. I would have stopped speaking to his ass then. You're too nice Shaunie. We need to find you a rich husband to spoil you," Liza says as she's pulling boxes off the shelves. Just as we finish counting all the boxes of messenger bags Naomi texted me. "Uh oh, it's Naomi. She's got info," I say, suddenly hyperventilating. "Oh shit! Okay calm down, breathe, and open it," Liza says trying to calm me down. I take a deep breath and open the text.

Naomi: *I have info are you ready?*

Me: *No, but go ahead.*

Naomi: *Are you sure? Maybe you should sit.*

Me: *Naomi my heart is in my throat. Just send it.*

One by one the pictures flooded my phone. Happy smiling pictures of him and his kids, him and her, him, her and their kids. There were pictures of him professing his love for her, pictures of them hugged up together, pictures of her grinning wearing a ring. She was wearing a ring on her fourth finger left hand. It was THE ring. I passed the phone to Liza and sat on one of the dusty messenger bag boxes. "For someone who doesn't use social media he sure knows how to make collages," Liza says. "You want to know a fun fact? Look at the date on the "love of my life" picture with all the hearts and shit." "Yes. What about it?" "It was posted a week after he met up with me to find my banquet dress," I say sulking. "That bastard! He's shopping with you while his wife is at home with the kids?" Liza says, pissed. "I let him draw in my foam," I say whining. "Excuse me?" "Cappuccinos Liza, we had cappuccinos that night. Ugh I'm sad," I say, letting out a big sigh.

Naomi: *Hello....*

Naomi: *Are you okay?*

Naomi: *Now what?*

Me: *Sorry Chica. I'm in a state of shock. I'm going to call you later. Tell Sissy I said great job and thank you.*

Naomi: *You should send him all those picture and tell him to kick rocks.*

Me: *IDK what to do.*

"Is it possible to get a copy of his marriage license? That's public records right?" I ask Liza. "What? I'm sure you can, but do you think he's worth all of that?" She was right. Just that quick I was becoming obsessed. One thing's for sure, he needs to know I know.

"So is he married?" Robyn asked over the phone. "I don't know for sure, but the woman was wearing a ring. It could be an engagement ring or a wedding band. It's hard to tell in the picture." "Well one thing for sure is those pictures confirm they are together. I can't believe he was teasing you about missing his birthday. He wanted to spend the day with you. Ha. Shouldn't she have planned something?" Robyn asked sarcastically. "Exactly, we talk about everything. Why couldn't he tell me that?" I say whining. "Correction kiddo YOU talk about everything. He talks about certain things," Robyn says. "I can't believe I felt so bad about missing his birthday. I was planning to take him out to make up for it. Maybe even get him a present," I say with a sigh. "You should frame those pictures and give that to him as a birthday present. Like, here Jerk-off, Happy Birthday," Robyn says laughing. "OMG this is why you're my best friend! You got knowledge!" "Put a bow on it," Robyn says and we both start laughing.

I decided to meet up with Raquel after work. We needed to catch up and do a little gift bag shopping. "I'm thinking about moving to California. They have nice weather, a cool job market, more living space, and more men," Raquel says. "All of that is probably true, but I love New York. Perhaps when I'm rich and famous I'll own a home somewhere hot, but my main residence will always be New York City. Now let's go to Job2 so we can organize our tiny ass living spaces and dress up my little gift," I say proudly. I found a small gift bag that fit the frame I purchased. "Oh look! This tissue paper has little dog paws on it," I say gushing. "Ha how fitting" Raquel says sarcastically. I now had everything I needed for Framed's late birthday gift. "Please can I go? I'll sit in the corner of the restaurant. You won't even know I'm there. I'm dying to see his reaction." "You sound like Robyn and Naomi. I will let you know how it goes. I need to do this on my own. I'm just waiting for him to be free for lunch," I say, followed by an evil laugh. Raquel joined me in my evil fairy tale queen laugh. "We seriously need help." "I know right," I say giggling.

Three weeks. I was cool, calm and collected for three weeks. I kept speaking with Framed and being nice. It was so natural with us. So normal to laugh and just talk. I would often forget about my plan so I kept the gift bag on my desk so I would remember. I didn't want to forget how he once again omitted information. I couldn't be nice. I had to show how disappointed I was. Finally, just when I thought I wouldn't be able to go through with it, Framed accepted my lunch offer. I told him it would be quick because I had work I needed to get done. He was okay with that as he had work as well.

Noon could not come fast enough. I grabbed the gift bag and went to meet him. He was late, coming from home, and had made time to see me before he went into work. I stood outside the diner practicing what I wanted to say. I would pass him the bag and say, "Hi! Care to explain this shit?" No, too harsh.

"Happy Birthday! How long have you been married?" No, too accusatory. Maybe I'll just pass him the bag and as he pulls out the frame I'll just stare and say, "Why?" Ooh I like that. Low key with a dramatic pause, this may work. I continue to think of what to say while this young, kind of attractive man asks me for directions. "Yes Macy's. It is that way. Keep going. It's maybe three more blocks. Just go that way." Maybe he was trying to flirt I don't know. I was focused on Framed and this guy needed to scram.

As the dude starts to walk away, I see Framed walking toward me. "Hello. Sorry I'm late. Framed says looking at the guy walking away, confused. "Hi. I was just giving directions. He had a hard time comprehending." "I can see that. Shall we go inside?" He opens the doors and we stand in the front and wait for a seat. "You look nice as always," Framed says as we take our seats. "Thank you, so do you," I say very blandly. I ordered tea and he ordered a Coke. I didn't want to eat because the knots in my stomach wouldn't let me. We were having a great time laughing and talking and I almost forgot his gift bag was sitting right next to me until he said, "You went shopping," he says eyeing the bag. "What? Oh no, no this is a gift. It's a gift for you actually. I felt bad I missed your birthday and I wanted to do something." "What? You know you didn't have to get me anything. You're too nice," Framed says taking the bag from me. "Yeah I know. I've been hearing that a lot lately. Open, Open, Open!" I say with excitement, clapping my hands.

My smile froze on my face as I watched him dig through all the dog paw print tissue paper. Despite knowing my plan and what my friends discovered, I was still having a great time at lunch with him. It sucks that his dishonesty had to ruin it. He pulled out the frame. With his jaw hitting the floor, sighing ever so deeply, he closed his eyes and his entire body sulked. I just sat there watching with my frozen smiling face. Honestly for three weeks I tried to be angry and mean, but I just couldn't. No feeling trumped the hurt and disappointment I felt in that very moment. "Why did you do this? Why didn't you just ask me? You don't understand," he says as he fumbled with his words. "If I did it any other way it wouldn't be me," I say with an innocent shoulder shrug. "You didn't have to do this. This was over the top. All you had to do was ask," he said, looking disappointed. "Yeah well it is what it is. Now tell me Framed, how long have you been married?" I said, as I pushed the tea cup away (in case he said the wrong thing and it "accidentally" fell in his lap from me knocking it over on purpose). "I am not married. I can't believe you did this. You just don't understand." "Why don't you help me understand? Here I am wondering why you are so vague, why won't you open up to me, thinking maybe I'm intimidating, seriously blaming myself, and all the while you've been with your children's mother, aka your best friend. Do you live together? Are you engaged?" I ask as I feel the anger intensifying. "Sometimes, but it's not what you think. We do not live together. We are not married." "Sometimes, what does that mean? You're not engaged all the time? That doesn't make any sense," I say pissed. "I really wished you would have just asked me," Framed says, looking at the bag. "I'm asking you now. What is going on?" I say leaning in. "We are on-again off-again. I told myself if any relationship was going to work, I would make sure it was the one with her. Sometimes we have good days, weeks, sometimes months, and then we don't. I'm trying to work it out, but she flips flops. I hurt her and I'm trying to right my wrong. I met you and you're my type. Smart, beautiful, ambitious. You're perfect. I got caught up, but I've always been very careful about not hurting you. That is the last thing I would ever want to do. I maintain a distance between us because I know the potential. When things are great with her I limit my communication and can't focus on having a great time with you. When things are great with you, things go bad with her. I am so sorry. You are amazing. You're it. This is why I don't date. I'm just in a messed up situation."

I could tell he was genuine and finally opening up. Yes I was disappointed, but I couldn't hate him. He was my friend and there was no denying our connection. At the end of our back and forth, I told him we could remain friends. It wouldn't be easy, but we could try. Knowing that I could never love a man whose heart belonged to someone else allowed me to let go of the idea of just dating him and letting the chips fall where they may. I actually felt bad for him. I always say when you forgive someone, you have to forgive wholeheartedly. A person shouldn't have to pay for their mistakes for the rest of their lives. Granted, I didn't know both sides of the story, he could have been a real ass to her, but either way, the back and forth was not fair to either of them.

Framed paid the bill and we left the diner. We decided to walk a little and try to get back to normal. We stood under some scaffolding and he reminded me of our fantasy trip to Barcelona. He'd imagined seeing me at a coffee shop wearing all white, and he would walk up behind me and greet me hello. We would be so happy together, knowing for sure that everything happened for a reason and we were meant to be. He knows how much I love that fairy tale shit. It made me smile even though I was still mad at him.

"I was so disappointed when my friend sent me all those pictures. It was like a shot was fired, each time one appeared on my phone. I had trouble deciding which one to frame. I figured I'd go with the one with the hearts since you made the effort to decorate it. Ugh I could punch you in the tummy right now," I say getting mad all over again. "If it makes you feel better go ahead. I hate that I made you feel like this. Go ahead punch me I can take it," opening his jacket. I gave a few gentle jabs. No physical pain could make him hurt the way I was hurting emotionally. "So the distance thing, that explains that funky phone number you gave me. I mean I have the job number, but so does Google. That phone number is an app. You purposely don't open that app sometimes huh? That's so messed up," I say putting my head down. "I know I'm sorry. I'll give you my number," Framed says "No keep it. I don't even want it now. I'm good. Listen I have to get back to work. I'm going to take the train back." "Wait let me walk you to your train," Framed says as he catches up to me. He grabbed my hand and interlocked our fingers as we crossed the street. When we got to the train station, he leaned up against the wall and pulled me close. He gently moved my hair away from my face and kissed me. It was so passionate my knees weakened. We couldn't care less who was watching. "Text me when you get to work please." "Text that fake phone number? No thanks I'll pass." I start going down the subway steps and I hear him yelling out his phone number repeatedly. I couldn't believe him. A huge smile came on my face, but I did not turn around. I threw up the peace sign and kept going. I had a train to catch.

#

Chapter 13: Deal or No Deal

My birthday was around the corner and I had no idea what I wanted to do. My friends kept asking, but sometimes I can't decide until the last minute. It's hard when your birthday falls in the middle of the week. Mine fell on a Wednesday this year. Everyone knows that Thursday is the new Friday and Friday is the new Saturday. As for Saturday and Sunday, those were brunch days. Not much going on hump day. What's a girl to do? I put in a request for a few days off at Job2. The one thing I was certain of was that I didn't want to bring in my birthday there. I wanted my feet to hurt because I was dancing the night away, not because I was standing, working the night away.

Framed and I were finally in a good place, a platonic friend good place. We still enjoyed each other's company from time to time, but we controlled ourselves. We stuck to our deal of never having sex and I was glad we did. I think if we hadn't, there wouldn't be a friendship at all.

Getting to a "good place" with Framed and still having love for him was not easy, that's for sure. I guess I never really allowed myself to be in a "bad place" with him. The thing with Framed was, I had stopped looking at him as a future mate the moment he made it clear he didn't want to have any more children. At least that's what I told myself over and over again. Was I hurt that he omitted information from me on more than one occasion? Was I hurt that I had to do research to get him to tell me the truth? I won't use the word hurt; I was more disappointed that it had to get to that point. The point of me giving him a framed picture of himself and his secret as a birthday gift in such a dramatic soap opera fashion (Emmy-worthy might I add). I would have rather had an honest conversation, but using the dramatics seemed to be the only way to get him to not dance around the truth. I guess I figured his honesty would help determine if we were destined to be together. Do I think we are compatible? Yes. Do I think we could have been something amazing, like an envied power couple? Oh hell yes. But I couldn't ignore the facts. He was a great guy that struggled with his loyalty to his children's mother, and let me reiterate how clear he was he didn't want any more children. As far as a romantic relationship is concerned, those are deal breakers.

He would never be able to adore me the way I deserve: I want someone 100 percent sure about me, and I won't allow any man to take away the option of experiencing motherhood. There are just some things in your heart you feel you are destined to be, and for me, being a mom is on my list.

Once I was able to accept Framed for who he was, I was unable to harbor anger toward him. I could accept that as long as he chooses to handle his personal situations the way he does, then he will never be more than a platonic friend to me. I won't lie; after speaking with him sometimes, I hope he realizes he deserves ultimate happiness. I sometimes hope he would want that kind of happiness with me. But according to my Chakra test results, my third eye is overactive and I need to chill out and not get so wrapped up in my fantasy world (who knew?).

I have made the choice to not be mad at people for not living up to my expectations of them. They are just that, "MY" expectations not theirs. I just throw my hands up and hope they realize there is more to life than what they allow themselves to partake in. I hope one day they see the greatness that I see in them. But what do I know, my third eye is out of control. So I told myself Framed was just a guy friend that I had a crush on and I guess I was just waiting for that "crush phase" to pass. It was not easy, but I felt the friendship was worth the effort.

Framed and I met up after work one evening and decided to take a little stroll. "So what are you doing for your birthday?" Framed asked. "I think I want to eat somewhere fun, but I'm not sure yet. If I do it would be on Sunday." "Copy. I'm going to be in the city Sunday. Where are you having it?" "Why? You can't come. You have to work," I say giving him the side eye. "I know, but who's to say I couldn't pop up?" Framed says smiling. "Me! I say you can't pop up. I'll pass on that idea," I say, playfully giving him a hard time. "Well I'm going to be traveling a lot for work. I'm headed to Chicago, Philly, and DC, helping my company open new stores out there. I'll be gone for a few weeks. Maybe you can visit me in DC?" Framed asks with a hopeful grin. "I love DC! We'll see. I'm focused on my birthday right now. I can't think that far ahead," I say, really considering going to DC. "Copy. Maybe we can catch a movie on Wednesday? I leave Thursday." "No I don't think that's a good idea. My actual birthday is Wednesday and if you're not going to make a grand gesture, I don't think we should hang out. I don't want to put that kind of pressure on you. After all it's not a regular day…just saying." Framed starts laughing, "Well thank you for the consideration." "Anytime!" I say, proud I was putting myself first.

I had finally decided that I wanted to have a birthday brunch; I liked the idea of my friends and I getting all dressed up and having a nice meal with unlimited mimosas and bellinis. The best part was everyone could have a great time and still be home at a decent hour to get ready for work on Monday. Birthday Brunch Bonus: I would get to wear my sparkly dress, which I had purchased to wear for New Year's 2015. Instead, I had stayed home, sipped champagne, and giggled at the *Honeymooners* in my pajamas. To be honest I didn't mind at all. I was drunk, warm, safe, and my feet were very comfortable in my fuzzy slippers. The days of staying out until 3 and 4 in the morning were long gone. Sometimes I feel like such an old lady; as soon as the sun goes down I'm already yawning.

"I got it! Brunch at PS 450, 4pm, and I'm keeping it small, only 15 people. What do you think?" I say to Robyn over the phone. "Cool I'm in. Let me put it in my uh oh." "What you mean uh oh?" I say waiting patiently for a good-ass excuse. "My nephew's birthday party is that day. It's in the boonies. I don't think I can make both." "Oh that's okay. Just send a nice gift. He's little. He won't know what's going on anyway," I say. "No I

221

don't think I'll be able to make your brunch. I RSVP'd weeks ago. By the time his party ends and I get all the way to Manhattan your brunch will be over," Robyn says whining. "GASP! You're going to miss your best friend's birthday. Miss your sister from another mister's life celebration? I can't even look at you right now!" I say in total shock. "We're on the phone. Stop being so extra! I will try my best to make it," Robyn says laughing. "No, no go play in the bouncy house. I'll live," I say calmly. "Good I'm glad you're accepting the news so well," Robyn says sarcastically. "No it's cool. We'll be friends forever. Even when we're 85 years old, sipping bellinis in our rocking chairs and laughing at old reruns of 'Sex and the City.' I'll lean over and say into your good ear, remember my 34th birthday brunch when we danced all afternoon and sipped bellinis? Oh wait, no you wouldn't remember, because YOU WEREN'T THERE!!!" I scream. After Robyn finished laughing at me she said, "I'm hanging up. I have to go teach class petty princess. Later, Chica." "Toodles noodles," I say and hang up the phone. I pulled my sparkly dress out of the closet. I was getting really excited about finally having a chance to wear it. I had just decided to try it on when I got a text from Naomi.

Naomi: *Hey baby cakes. I miss your guts. What are the b-day plans?*

Me: *Hey sunshine. I've decided to have brunch at PS.450 on Sunday. Make sure you tell Sissy. You can make it right? No flaking.*

Naomi: *We're going to be there. I promise. I missed your b-day one time. Give me a break.*

Me: *Yeah well Robyn is competing with your track record. It's the same day as her nephew's b-day party. She has to go she RSVP'd.*

Naomi: *She is never going to hear the end of this one.*

Me: *LOL you know me so well.*

Naomi: *LOL be nice.*

The more I twirled around in my dress the more excited I became. I was about to be 34 years old and I wasn't doing badly in life. I have a fun career, my own place, my own car, and my own sense of self. I am grateful to have such wonderful friends and family, and I am healthy, strong and independent. I am truly blessed. I've finally started to accept the things I have, rather than worry about the things I don't. Speaking of don't: I grabbed my phone and typed into my calendar: Don't forget to buy nude Spanx. Phew! I can't believe I almost forgot about that. I mean I was hitting the gym quite often these days, but I wasn't giving up my pizza and wine nights. Nothing was going to jiggle on its own in that dress.

"So how was your birthday brunch princess?" Sasha asked as I walked up to the reception desk. "It was awesome. I love it when the people I show up for show up for me. My best friend Ryan took me to dinner on my actual birthday. He never lets me go the day of without a plan. We even went to Dylan's Candy Shop. We always have a great time doing the simplest things," I say smiling. "AWW that's so sweet. Sounds like you should be dating him," Sasha says smiling. "You sound like my family. Don't start. Anyhoo, brunch was great. I have no idea how many bellinis I had, but everyone had a great time and that is what matters most to me. I love that all my friends get along so nicely." I was beaming. "That's because good people attract other good people. It makes total sense," Sasha says. "Girl, what did I tell you about making me blush like that; I have to get back to work. Travel season is upon us," I say, flaring my arms as I walk away. "You're so silly. I'll harass you later!" Sasha yells.

Let the traveling begin. It was time to city hop with the wine tour and we were headed to Chicago, Las Vegas, and Dallas. I'd never been to Dallas so I wanted it to be memorable. The headquarters for Job2 was located in Dallas, and as luck would have it, a few people from our Dallas location were in town. They were building fixtures for the store the night I was scheduled to work. When I asked who had the best barbecue in Dallas, the vote was unanimous. Pecan Lodge was where my co-workers and I would dine our first night in the Cowboy's city. Liza was on board: she had checked the menu in advance and had her mind set on their southern fried chicken. I on the other hand had my mind set on dessert, so their homemade peach cobbler was on my radar. I have a major sweet tooth. We got to the hotel around 1pm, and the restaurant closed at 3pm. To me this meant it was the real deal and we had to hurry. Dallas was the last stop on the tour and the most dreaded, since the hotel was in the middle of nowhere. We called a cab and were off.

I have to say this dining experience with my co-workers had to be the funniest event. My boss was comical; like Alexis Carrington of *Dynasty* meets *Green Acres*. We let my boss order the food: "Hi. We would like a half-pound of the ribs, the brisket, the pulled pork, fried chicken, mac and cheese, coleslaw, and for dessert, peach cobbler and banana pudding. Thank you."

The lady behind the register says, "Is that order just for you? That's not enough food for 4 people." My boss says, "Why not? We're from New York. We don't eat like this normally. The four of us have split a steak." My co-workers and I are in tears, trying to hold in our laughter. "Ma'am we sell the meat by the pound. You're basically getting 2 pieces of everything and 2 very small sides." "Oh I see, well just double the order," my boss says to the woman, then turns to us and says, "I don't know how to order cooked meat by the pound." I burst into laughter. I couldn't hold it anymore. The crazy thing was, after she ordered the ribs all I kept thinking was: one rib? We each get one rib? My co-workers and I still tease my boss about trying to eat a rib with a knife and fork. She was a good sport and laughed at herself. It was certainly an interesting experience and the food was absolutely amazing.

When I got back home after all that traveling, I needed to get myself back on a schedule. All the time zone differences really messed up my eating habits and workout routine. For the past two years I'd been saying that I wanted to become a runner, so I guess there was no time like the present.

An old college friend of mine had been running for years, and had just moved back to the east coast. He said he would help me get into the swing of things, and kept his promise. When I told him I was ready, he came all the way from Jersey to teach me proper running techniques in Van Cortlandt Park. What I learned quickly was that running on concrete and running on the treadmill are two very different things. I bragged all day long how

I ran on the treadmill for 30-40 minutes at a time. I just knew running outside would be no different. After a light jog of 2 minutes, I was winded and ready to go home. "Go, go on without me," I gasped, while waving my arm as I hunched over to breathe. "This is not a horror movie. Stop telling me to go on and save myself," he would say laughing at me. He certainly had the patience of a saint. He taught me to pace myself: I would run for 2 minutes straight as fast as I could, then walk for 1 minute to catch my breath. Eventually I started to extend the minutes I was running.

Running became my new interest. I loved being outside as the scenery was always different. To my left I would see guys playing soccer; to my right people were playing tennis. There were a lot of bike riders, which made me start thinking about purchasing one myself. There were people just sitting on the lawn having a picnic and kids running around playing catch. I enjoyed each scene as I ran passed it. I started running everywhere as I built more stamina. I discovered a track right near my apartment. I had lived there for almost 4 years and never knew about this track. It was huge and split into different pathways. Every time I ran on the track, I started at the same spot, but I would always take a different path, discovering more beautiful sides to my neighborhood. My mom started joining me on my runs. They turned into power walks with her, but I loved it. She was taking her health seriously and I was very proud of her.

One day out of the blue, Framed contacted me, He had the weekend off, which was rare and was spending it with his kids. He knew that running was becoming a part of my new healthy lifestyle and wanted to join me. He was an athlete in high school and wanted to get back in shape. He found a really nice park for us to run in, and I agreed to meet him at 9am on a Sunday morning. I decided to wear a cute running outfit. I knew I would be sweating and my hair would look a mess, but at least my running ensemble would be well put-together.

I pulled into the parking area of the park and Framed was standing there by his truck, smiling. I parked next to him. He came over, opened my door, helped me out the car, and kissed me. "Good morning. I like your running gear," he says holding onto my waist. "Really? Thanks, I was rushing and just threw this on," I say collecting myself from that knee-weakening kiss. What the hell happened to platonic? Jesus take the wheel.

Since Framed claimed he was rusty, I taught him the run 2 minutes, walk 1 minute method. He did way better than he thought he would. We got so into it we started racing. People were yelling "beat him, beat him go, go, go!" Goes to show, you should always do your best. You never know who is watching or who you may be inspiring.

Framed had also brought his basketball with him. We had spotted the basketball court on our first go-around the park. After our third run around, he actually wanted to stop at the court and play. I didn't run and bounce the ball like he did; my hand eye coordination is a little off. Having a game of one-on-one was going to be hilarious. Once I got the dribbling of the ball and running thing going, I was all over the place, shooting the ball like a pro (well, at least in my head I felt like a pro). If chasing me around with the ball wasn't exercise enough, laughing at me certainly burned any remaining calories for Framed.

As we walked back to the car, I gave him his props for being a skilled player and showing good sportsmanship. "This was so much fun. I love spending time with you. I like that we were able to do something different like this. Not so traditional you know?" Framed says. "Yeah me too, I had a good time. Basketball is harder than I remember as a kid. It got real a few times. The look in your eyes got a little crazy. In fact it made me nervous. I stopped trying to guard you so much. I'm too cute to get elbowed and knocked to the ground," I say wiping sweat off my forehead. Framed just laughed and shook his head.

When we got back to our cars we continued our chat. He gets into the driver seat of his truck and starts playing with his music, looking for something. I leaned in to give him a sweaty hug, laid my head on his chest and he held me there. All of a sudden Sam Smith starts playing. "Is his album good? I like him, I just haven't purchased it yet," I say to Framed. "It's a great album. I listen to it every time I leave you. A lot of the songs remind me of us." As I continue to enjoy our embrace I start to listen to the words and then I hear him hum and I can't stop smiling. When the song ends I pull away and say, "That was really nice, especially when you started humming." "Was I really?" he says shocked. He stops the CD, puts it in its case and hands it to me. "I want you to have it. I have another one at home. Listen to it and let me know what songs remind you of us." "Okay I will.

I'm going to head out. I need to eat and rest up for Monday," I say, smiling at the CD. He opens my car door, kisses me goodbye, and closes the door. Me being the eager beaver I am, I put in that CD immediately and listened to it all the way home. I parked my car and I texted Robyn right away.

Me: *I still love him!*

Robyn: *LMAO I freaking knew it.*

Me: *LOL whatever. We ran and played basketball.*

Robyn: *Oh Lord he Love and Basketballed you. Are you all hot and sweaty for real now?*

Me: *Yes and he gave me a CD.*

Robyn: *You two are cute, confusing, but super cute.*

Me: *I know right!!!*

  My summer seemed to be fairly quiet. I was still working 2 jobs and I hardly socialized. I had lunches here and there, but my focus was to save money and cut costs. I wrote that in my 2015 goals letter on New Year's Eve. I wrote quite a few goals in that letter now that I think about it (the more champagne I sipped the longer the list became). The list included things like: make the gym a part of my daily routine, read more books, see a play, become a millionaire, fall in love. You know, simple things like that. I had sealed it up and put it into my safe. "You can't open it until next New Year's Eve," my friend Miranda had told me about writing goal letters. She said it would be fun to open the letter after a year and see what I had accomplished on the list. And it would be okay to add whatever I had missed to the list again for the following year, along with new goals. She said she did it every year. It was tradition for her. It seemed like such a cool idea, that I had to try it. This way I would put some pressure on myself to achieve my life goals and keep my promise to myself to become the best possible me.

Miranda and our mutual friend Todd got tickets to go to a taping of the *T.D. Jakes Show*. They were filming in New York and the show would only broadcast in the south. Anyone who knows me knows how much I love Bishop T.D. Jakes. T.D. has a way of preaching that just speaks to your soul. After one of his sermons, you want to change your whole life around and just be better. Miranda and Todd had a great time. Miranda even got an autographed copy of his new book "Destiny." She was so excited about the experience, she told me I should go. She gave me the email to contact the studio and I wrote to them immediately. I was so excited when I got the email confirmation that my request for 3 tickets was accepted. I contacted my mom and told her to ask a friend. We kept laughing about taking the day off from work to be on television. Good thing it would only air in the south. Not sure how I would explain being too sick to come to work, but not too sick to be dressed up on television. I always have a good time with my mom so I was definitely looking forward to it.

Framed was traveling again for work and this time he was back in DC for a week. The invitation to visit was still open, but I wasn't sure if that was a good idea. We kept calling each other "just friends" but the attraction was getting harder and harder to ignore. Framed texted me that he was in the city for the day. He had meetings all morning and in the afternoon he was heading back to DC, but asked if I was free for lunch. I had made plans to leave work early that day so it worked out perfect. We went to Kabooz, a bar inside Penn Station. I had a cute lemon cocktail and he had scotch. "Come to DC with me," Framed says. "When, aren't you about to leave?" I ask confused. "Now, come with me today. Take Amtrak with me. You said you love the train ride to DC so come.". "Like with no bag of stuff, just go to DC for the night?" I ask sipping the hell out of that cocktail. "If you want, but I was thinking you could come back on Saturday with me," he says smiling. "Oh no, no, no, I'm not missing my chance to be on Jesus TV," I say. Clearly the cocktail had kicked in. "Whose TV?" Framed asks laughing. "I mean the Bishop T.D. Jakes has a talk show and I have tickets to be in the audience. I'm not missing that. Not to mention there is alternate side parking so I have to move my car. I don't think this is going to happen," I say watching him type on his laptop. "Oh I see. Well, you don't have to miss the show. You just have to come back early in the morning that's all. I'll pay for the ticket on the car, so don't worry about that. Damn my train is booked." "Oh well wasn't meant to be," I say shrugging my shoulders. "Nope, look there's a train exactly 1 hour after mine. Let's book it," he says smiling. "Yeah that's great, but it's the return I'm worried about," I say rolling my eyes. "The earliest is a 4:30am. You'll be back in Penn Station by 7:45am. Is that enough time?" Framed says smiling. "Yes I suppose it is. This is crazy. I'm all for spontaneity and all but..."

"Just book it and tell me how much it cost okay. I'll see you in 5 hours? I have to go before I miss my train." Framed says interrupting my excuse. All I kept thinking was: what the hell did I just agree to?

Of course now I'm in panic mode. I have 45 minutes to buy toiletries, pajamas, and undies. Good thing my hair was in a bun and I always carry my brush in my bag. "Okay Shaunie you are absolutely crazy," I say out loud as I look through the racks of H&M. Ooh these are cute pajamas. Tank and boy shorts, that's perfect. Sexy but still covered. Nothing was going to happen anyway. Aunt Flow always seems to know when to show up when it comes to that man. The signs don't lie. No cookie for him. As I leave H&M after making my purchases, I head to Duane Reade. I'm waiting to cross the street and a homeless lady sitting in front of the store screams, "DON'T PUT IT IN YOUR MOUTH!" My eyeballs almost popped out of my head; I never said I was putting anything in my mouth. What was more troubling was I didn't know why I thought she was talking to me. I was looking around and it didn't appear that anyone else heard her, just me. I had to laugh. I know God speaks to you, you just have to listen. That right there was on a whole other level of communication. I get to Duane Reade and find a cute toiletry travel set and purchase some trail mix and water. You're living Shaunie! You're being spontaneous and grabbing the bull by the balls, horns, bull's balls? This is bullshit! I have lost my mind. I'm getting reimbursed like it's a business trip. What has this man done to me?

The train ride was beautiful as always. My phone was

plugged in so I was texting like crazy. I had to inform someone of my whereabouts. It was the responsible thing to do after all. Who better to tell than my girls?

Me: *Guess where I am.*

Robyn: *Oh no.*

Naomi: *What did you do?*

Me: *Pardon me. You two have no faith in my good judgment.*

Robyn: *Yeah so where are you?*

Naomi: *Shaunie you better say you're at the gym.*

Me: *Nope I'm heading to DC to hang out with Framed and then I'm coming home in the morning.*

Robyn: *Holy shit.*

Naomi: *I cannot believe you.*

Me: *I'm living. I'm young grabbing bull's balls. It's going to be great.*

Robyn: *Please text me when you get there and get back.*

Naomi: *This is why you're my favorite. You're fucking crazy. Be safe and he better meet you at the station.*

Me: *Yes we're meeting. I'll keep you two posted. I'm going to finish watching The Wedding Ringer.*

Okay, can I just say *The Wedding Ringer* was hilarious? I totally have to watch it again, but uninterrupted. The movie kept getting interrupted by Framed's texts. He was asking my location and what wine I liked. He must have something up his sleeve; we only had about 7 hours there and he needed to make every hour count. I arrive and Framed is there to greet me with a big hug and kiss. "I wanted to get you flowers, but I was rushing trying to get the wine and the place didn't sell flowers. I'm sorry," he says hugging me again. "It's okay. I'm happy I came. It's a beautiful night," I say, looking around. "I know, especially since you're here. Are you hungry?" Framed asks. "I'm always hungry. I don't want anything too fancy though. I'm not really dressed for that. Let's keep it simple." "I know exactly where to take you. I go here a lot. The food is really good and it's a nice crowd." We walk one block to the restaurant. We get inside and it's not much of a crowd. It was about 10pm. We were right in downtown DC, but I guess Thursday is not the new Friday out there. Framed ordered us a pitcher of sangria and the waitress recommended her favorite dish, their shrimp and pasta. Framed switched my protein to chicken because of my shellfish allergy and I blushed that he remembered. Framed was so relaxed in DC. He was fun and carefree. It was so nice to see him not rush. The food was great and the sangria was very yummy. He paid the bill and it was time to go to his place. We walked across the street and entered this beautiful building. "This is where they put you?" I say with my eyes wide open. "Yes," he said with a chuckle. We get into the elevator and he presses the PH button. "So I got us some white wine. I figured we could enjoy it on the roof top." "WHY are you acting like you didn't just hit the button for the Penthouse? They put you in a Penthouse? You're acting like you do this shit EVERY DAY," I scream. Framed could not stop laughing. "Well you know eh em I'm a boss," and we both start laughing hysterically. We get to his penthouse suite and it is absolutely gorgeous. He instructs me to put my bag anywhere as he grabs the wine, two wine glasses, and we head back out. "I'll give you a tour when we get back. I'm anxious for you to see this view," he says pushing for the special elevator that goes to the rooftop.

When the elevator doors open my jaw drops. It is breathtaking. There are couches and chaise lounges everywhere, beautiful plants scattered all over, and votive candles on the tables. He took my hand and guided me to the edge. DC was gorgeous all lit up. "You really don't understand how happy I am to share this with you. I'm in my favorite city with my favorite person. Thank you so much for coming," he says, not breaking eye contact. He opened the wine and we toasted to our beautiful night in DC. We sipped a little and well, then it was on. He pulled me close to him and somehow I ended up straddling him. He slapped me on my butt and kissed me. When he had enough of the chair action, he lifted me up and pinned me to the wall. Someone must have been lifting weights because he lifted with ease and I know I'm no lightweight. He kept trying to open my pants, but I had informed him of Aunt Flow before I got there. I guess me continuously placing his hands elsewhere really turned him on because the grips got tighter, kisses more passionate, and the bites were harder. Aunt Flow certainly saved our friendship once again, because had she not been there, that would have been my first time getting some on a rooftop. Sex on the roof would count as a deal breaker. After about an hour and a half, we wore each other out with the teenage love affair behavior. We regained our composure, and sipped and talked some more. I couldn't believe I was here and with him. It felt so right.

We went back down to the penthouse holding hands. He gave me a tour of his temporary home and made sure he kissed me in every room. We finally lay in the bed and well it was on once again. All I kept hearing in my head was, "Don't put it in your mouth!" I tried to ignore it, but I couldn't and burst into laughter as he kissed my neck. When I told him what the women shouted out, he could not stop laughing. "Why the hell would she say that? She ruined everything now!" he says and I couldn't stop laughing. We ended up falling asleep for about two hours and then our alarms went off. It was time for me to get ready to leave. He kept asking me to stay, but I wasn't missing my 15 minutes of fame. Plus my mom was really excited to go. He arranged an Uber and walked me downstairs. He kissed and held me like he didn't want to let go, but I couldn't stay. I had to get back to my responsibilities.

I got on my train and as soon as I found a seat he called me. We talked for about an hour, but we both needed sleep. I tried to sleep on the train, but I'm always afraid some crazy person is going to get on and cause a scene, or worse some crazy person with body odor would get on and sit next to me. I napped in between stops while trying to watch *The Wedding Ringer* again.

Before I knew it I was back home, moving my car, avoiding a ticket, hurrying to take another shower and getting dressed for the show. I met my mom on the subway. She looked so cute wearing her curly hair. "What's up kiddo? How was your night?" she asked. "Oh it was cool. I went to DC," I say very nonchalantly. "Oh Okay! YOU WHAT?" she yelled.

The T.D. Jakes Show was amazing. I'm so happy we were able to be in the audience. Of course after watching the guests' breakthroughs and uplifting stories, I became very inspired to stick with my goal list. Falling in love is something I thought would be easy since I wear my heart on my sleeve, but nope, not easy at all. Yes, it can be a goal, but it is not something you can schedule. I honestly think I hadn't fallen in love yet because I wasn't ready for it. I want to be completely whole before I can even wrap my head around dating someone seriously.

I want to give 100 percent, because that's what I expect in return. I started thinking about the guys I had attracted over the years. Some were spoiled, selfish, financially unstable, confused, arrogant, greedy, mama's boys, or just plain unavailable. I know like attracts like, but there were definitely some opposites attract moments throughout the years as well. Perhaps a couple just had bad timing and we would be able to try again when the timing was right. One thing I knew for sure is that settling was not an option. All I can do is continue to work on being the person God intended me to be, and everything that is meant for me will be for me.

A few weeks later, I finally decided to make an appointment and see about trading in my car. The past winter I was slipping and sliding all over the place but that was not happening this winter. Shaunie was getting All-Wheel Drive. Take that wintry mix! I kept in mind that I wanted to cut costs, but I needed an SUV or, at the very least, a crossover vehicle.

When I got to the dealership I looked a mess. My hair was thrown up in a messy bun. I wasn't wearing any make-up and I had on sweats. I was not in the mood for the niceties and schmoozing. I had been there, done that. With experience under my belt, there was no way I was going to be swindled. "Hello Shaunie, it's very nice to meet you. My name is TheDealer," the sales guy says with his hand out. I gave the firmest handshake I could. "Hello nice to meet you." "That's a good grip you have. I like that. You mean business," TheDealer says. "Oh I'm focused. I know exactly what I want," I say. "Good because I want to give you exactly what you want," The Dealer says smiling.

After I explain everything I am looking for in a new vehicle, including what features were most important, he began to run the facts and figures. While we waited for the results we talked about my career and what I like to do for fun. Then we ended up talking about family and it turned out his niece was around the same age as my nephew. Then I can't even tell you how I ended up talking to him about my online dating shenanigans. It was like I was on stage. The Dealer could not stop laughing. "You should write a book. Shaun, you are hilarious," The Dealer says, wiping his eyes. Did he just call me Shaun like he's known me for years? He gets the figures back and I don't like them. He tells me to come back in October when they have this super sale and I'll get more bang for my buck. I agree to wait and he walked me to my car. "Shaunie you are absolutely gorgeous. You are so smart and so funny. I already have your number, but I was wondering if you would give me permission to use it?" he says. I was so caught off guard. Now

I'm not looking at him like he's a sales guy; now I'm looking at a potential date. I gave him a quick body scan. He was tall, clean cut, handsome, employed, funny, and the coolest part, he wanted to get to know me even though I looked like a piping hot mess. There's nothing wrong with making a new friend right? "Um sure, yeah, I'd like that," I say trying to fix my hair. "Good! Maybe I could end your dating horror stories. How's that sound?" The Dealer says. "Sounds like a deal!" I say as I get in my car and drive off.

I find it funny how when you are looking to be in a relationship, everyone seems coupled up and taken. When you don't think about "the hunt," people just start falling into your lap. What was weird to me was I wasn't interested in being in a relationship and it was no longer a high priority. I was over it and needed space. I really just wanted to enjoy time by myself and looked forward to getting to know me better. I don't know all the wonderful things God has in store for me, but I do find comfort in knowing HIS plan is better than mine. My dreams and vivid imagination confirm that.

I decided to take the time alone to think and have my next decision be the right decision. With that being said, I quit Job2. I learned all I needed to know and it was time to move on.

People say it's not until you step out of your comfort zone that you know what you are truly made of. Well, the last time I stepped out of mine I wrote a book. God is good.

The ~~End~~ Beginning!

#

Epilogue

Thank you for reading *Diving In Stilettos First*. I hope you enjoyed it and were able to not only laugh, but take away a few lessons from my mistakes. When I first started writing this book, I thought it would just be interesting to see all my dating woes written out. Surely I couldn't be the only lady having these wacky dating experiences.

As I continued to write, my perspective changed. I started realizing behaviors and patterns not just with the men I dated, but with myself. This book became therapeutic for me and when I took a moment and read how everything played out, it definitely gave me a reality check. It was clear I needed to change my ways, so that I could start attracting what's best for me. Not just with dating, but with life in general.

I hope this book inspired you to want more for yourself, be more confident, and become your best you. Everyone should experience euphoria in their lifetime, and it all starts with loving yourself first and knowing you deserve the very best.

I'm a proud work-in-progress!

Toodles Noodles xoxo

Works Cited

1 Cutrone, Kelly and Meredith Bryan. *If You Have to Cry, Go Outside: And Other Things Your Mother Never Told You* New York: Harper Collins Publishers (2010, December 28). Print

2 Harvey, S. [Steve Harvey]. "You don't lose a good man, you lose a man who's not good for you!" #SteveHarveyTV (2013, September 17). Tweet https://twitter.com/IAmSteveHarvey/status/380122534487670788?lang=en

3 Haynes, Jr., Cornell [aka Nelly]. "Two is not a winner and 3 nobody remembers."
"#1" from *Nellyville*. Universal Records, 2002. Compact Disc.

4 Jakes, T.D. [T.D. Jakes]. "You'd be surprised at the things that look great on the outside but are dysfunctional on the inside. Be sure to function as good as you look."
T.D. Jakes Ministries. (2013, November 20). Facebook Post https://www.facebook.com/bishopjakes/posts/10152133408733322

5 Sternberg, Thomas. (Producer) & Wells, Audrey. (Producer/Director/Screenwriter).
Under the Tuscan Sun. Touchstone Pictures USA / Italy (2003). Film.

All text messages quoted throughout are verbatim, including any errors in grammar and spelling.

Diving in Stilettos Inspiration

Have you ever heard a song and it takes you back to a certain place in time? Well listed below are a few songs that remind me of my time with Mr. Right Now. This list was just to name a few. There are so many more. ☺

Vegas
"Mr. Know it All" sung by Kelly Clarkson

Can'tGetRight
"Ain't Nothin' Goin' on But the Rent" sung by Gwen Guthrie

Bagel Boy
"Who is She 2 U" sung by Brandy

Superman
"Next Lifetime" sung by Erykah Badu

StickyFingers
"Raise Your Glass" sung by Pink

AppleBee'sKing /Chef OnALedge/Dr. NoNotReally
"Someone to Call My Lover" sung by Janet Jackson

DramaKing
"You Gets No Love" sung by Faith Evans

StrawSipper
"You're Not My Kind of Girl" sung by New Edition (Swap girl for boy)

Framed
"Good Thing" sung by Sam Smith

Diablo
"Stronger" sung by Kelly Clarkson